Hands-on Culture of Ancient Greece and Rome

Kate O'Halloran

J. WESTON

WALCH

PUBLISHER

Portland, Maine

Dedication

παρα εμηυ θυγατερα

User's Guide
to
Walch Reproducible Books

As part of our general effort to provide educational materials which are as practical and economical as possible, we have designated this publication a "reproducible book." The designation means that purchase of the book includes purchase of the right to limited reproduction of all pages on which this symbol appears:

Here is the basic Walch policy: We grant to individual purchasers of this book the right to make sufficient copies of reproducible pages for use by all students of a single teacher. This permission is limited to a single teacher, and does not apply to entire schools or school systems, so institutions purchasing the book should pass the permission on to a single teacher. Copying of the book or its parts for resale is prohibited.

Any questions regarding this policy or requests to purchase further reproduction rights should be addressed to:

Permissions Editor
J. Weston Walch, Publisher
321 Valley Street • P. O. Box 658
Portland, Maine 04104-0658

1   2   3   4   5   6   7   8   9   10
ISBN 0-8251-3741-1

Contents

Illustration Credits

A Coloring Book of Ancient Greece, Bellerophon Books, Santa Barbara, CA

      page 2   *Oedipus and the Sphinx*, from a red-figure amphora by the Achilles Painter; Boston, Museum of Fine Arts.

      page 15   *A Greek Scribe*

      page 26   *Demeter, goddess of the harvest*, from a red-figure skyphos by Makron; British Museum, London.

      page 28   *An Ancient Dance*, from a Corinthian black-figure cup in the National Museum, Copenhagen.

      page 34   *A Vase Painter at Work*, from a red-figure hydria by the Leningrad Painter; Torno Collection, Milan.

      pages 36, 37   *Duck and Griffin*, from an East Greek oinochoe in the Antikensammlungen, Munich.

      page 40   *Two Lions*, from a red-figure oinochoe by the Dutuit Painter; Paris, Petit Palais.

Life in Ancient Greece, Dover Publications, Inc., New York

      pages 8, 15

Life in Ancient Rome, Dover Publications, Inc., New York

      pages 47, 52, 55, 57

Clip Art Book of Designs, Crescent Books, New York

      page 51

Subject Area Correlation

	SOCIAL STUDIES	ENGLISH	SCIENCE	ART	MATH
The City-States of Greece	x			x	
The Beginnings of Democracy	x			x	
Trials and Time	x		x	x	
Alpha, Beta, Alphabet	x	x	x	x	x
It's Greek to Me	x	x			
Greek Gods and Goddesses	x	x		x	
Greek Myths	x	x		x	
Tragedy and Comedy	x	x		x	
Potted History	x		x	x	
Homes and Mosaics in Ancient Athens	x			x	
Fabulous Frescoes	x			x	
Writing in Ancient Rome	x	x		x	
Games of Ancient Rome	x			x	x
Living Latin	x	x			
Food in Old Rome	x		x		
Roman Proverbs and Sayings	x	x			
Roman Numerals	x				x
A Roman Calculator	x	x		x	x

How to Use This Book

This book, like the others in the *Hands-on Culture* series by J. Weston Walch, Publisher, has been designed to help middle school teachers integrate the study of a culture into the curriculum. Textbooks can teach students about the history and geography of an area, but to gain any real understanding, students must also be exposed to the art and traditions of a culture. *Hands-on Culture of Ancient Greece and Rome* provides 18 ready-to-use activities to help you do just that. Through the projects in this book, students will be exposed to the Greek alphabet, mosaics in ancient Athens, Roman food, the art of the fresco, Greek gods and goddesses, games played in old Rome, and more.

Most of the projects in this book work well either as individual projects or as group activities. You should read both the teacher notes and student pages completely before presenting the activity to students. When a project requires setting up a work station, as in the fresco and cooking projects, you may find it best to divide the class into groups and set up several work areas. You may also find a group approach helpful for some of the other projects. As students deal with such unfamiliar material as the Greek alphabet, they may find it less intimidating to work together to find solutions. Unfamiliar words are defined in the glossary at the back of this book.

By their nature, all these projects are interdisciplinary. All are appropriate for a social studies class. Most are appropriate for an art class. Some activities are also appropriate for other subject areas; the correlation chart on page *v* presents these links. Some activities could be done in several different classes. The Roman calculator activity on page 64 is a good example. The background for this activity could be given in a social studies class, the math content could be explained in math class, and the calculator could be made in art class. If you are teaching about Greece and Rome as part of an interdisciplinary team, each teacher can teach the activities appropriate to his or her domain.

All the projects have been structured so that the teacher presenting the activity does not need to know either the historical context for an activity or the procedure for doing the project. Full background details are provided where needed. You can share some or all of this information with students if you wish, but it is not necessary for student completion of the project. The step-by-step student instructions for the activities should need no other explanation. All activities have been tested with middle school and high school students.

To help demonstrate the process, you may find it helpful to keep one or two examples of student work for each activity. The next time you present the activity, show the student work as models. When encountering unfamiliar material, students like to have a general idea of what is expected of them. I hope that you and your students enjoy this book, and that it helps deepen your students' understanding and appreciation of the cultures of ancient Greece and Rome.

Note: In some activities, including those on democracy and trial by jury, the pronoun "he" is used throughout. This is because citizenship was limited to free males of Athenian descent. Therefore, members of the Assembly or of a jury were always—and exclusively—male.

The City-States of Greece

OBJECTIVES

Social Studies

- Students will understand the key role of geography in the development of Greece.
- Students will be familiar with the location and characteristics of some of the principal Greek city-states.
- Students will be able to locate Greek city-states on a map.

Art

- Students will create a game board based on the Greek city-states.

MATERIALS

The City-States of Greece handout
map of modern Greece
poster board
pencils, paints, markers, other art supplies
dice
counters or other small objects to use as playing pieces
optional: book of Greek designs and motifs, samples of other board games like Monopoly™, Chutes and Ladders™, By Jove™, etc.

BACKGROUND

The land of Greece is divided by rugged mountains and many bays into small, isolated regions. Over time, independent city-states, or *poleis*, developed in separate regions. While there were some 300 poleis in all, Athens, Sparta, and Corinth were the most important ones.

Rivalries between the city-states were common. Different cities formed alliances with each other, then changed the alliances as circumstances changed. The rivalry between Athens and Sparta was the most important one; it led finally to the fall of Athens.

PROCEDURE

1. Distribute the handout and divide students into groups of three or four. Direct students to locate on a map of modern Greece each of the cities mentioned in the handout.

2. If you wish, show students the board for a game like Monopoly, and analyze the way the board is structured: All players start at the same point and move around the board by throwing the dice; different points around the board offer penalties and rewards.

3. Direct students to develop a board game for two to four players that shows the routes between Greek city-states. They will use the map of ancient Greece to plan routes. Point out that the sea routes will be the most straightforward, but that land routes are also possible, merely more difficult. The paths they plot from city to city should take into account the potential alliances and rivalries among the cities. Hazards can be adapted from Greek mythology: the riddling sphinx, the chimera, Scylla and Charybdis, the Oracle at Delphi, Mount Olympus, etc. Each group should create a complete game board and full written rules for playing the game.

4. When all game boards are completed, have a Greek City-States Game Day. Set up a table for each game, and have students play each other's games.

Oedipus and the sphinx

The City-States of Greece

Look at a map of modern Greece. What do you see? The area we call Greece is not one solid area. It is made up of many islands and peninsulas, and is surrounded by seas. Even where there is a large area of land, it is broken up by mountains. By nature, the area is divided into small, separate regions.

The civilization we know as **Classical Greece** began to develop around 800 B.C. But it didn't develop as one kingdom, with a shared government and laws. Instead, it developed as a patchwork of separate states—about 300 of them in all. Each of these independent states consisted of a town or city and the area immediately around the city. The Greek name for a **city-state** was *polis*.

Most of the city-states had a similar structure. At the center of the *polis* was a fortified hill. A temple to the city's patron deity was built on top of the hill. An area of flat ground around the hill was enclosed within a protective wall. Private houses were built inside this enclosed area. An area known as the *agora* acted as a market and general meeting place. The countryside outside the wall was used for farming.

All the city-states shared the same language and had a similar culture. But each state also had its own distinct nature.

Sparta

Sparta was the center of the area known as Lacedaemon. This area consisted of two plains bounded by mountain ranges. The city was never known as a place of beautiful buildings and fine statues. Very few poets or artists came from Sparta. Spartan society was built around the army. At the age of seven, boys were taken away from their families. They were sent to live in the soldiers' barracks, where they were trained to be cunning, tough, and strong. At 18, they began an intensive military training, and at 20 they became eligible to fight. Although Spartan men could marry at 20, they still had to live at the barracks. Only after the age of 30 were they allowed to leave the barracks and live with their wives. Girls stayed at home and learned housekeeping skills. One reason for this military society was fear that their slaves, the helots, would rise up against them. Spartans were fiercely proud. They were enemies of the Athenians, and would make alliances with other city-states against Athens.

Athens

The city-state of Athens was the largest in Greece. The area controlled by Athens was called Attica. At its center was a fortified hill called the Acropolis. Athens was a center of art and science. Athenian boys were taught to read and write, to do math, and to speak well in public. They were also taught to think for themselves. In school, boys memorized the poetry of Homer and learned to play the lyre, a musical instrument. At 18, they went to military school for two years. Meantime, girls were taught at home to be good wives and mothers. The city of Athens was famed for its literature, poetry, drama, theater, buildings, and government. Athenians prided themselves on being courteous and witty. They and the Spartans were enemies.

(continued)

The City-States of Greece *(continued)*

Corinth

The coastal city-state of Corinth had a glorious history as a busy trade center. In fact, the citizens of Corinth were so busy selling and buying that they sometimes hired others to fight for them. Although their schools were not as fine as those of Athens, boys in Corinth received a good education. From the ages of 7 to 14 they attended schools near their homes where they memorized poetry and studied drama, public speaking, reading, writing, math, and the flute. The sons of wealthy parents also attended a higher school. All boys then went to military school for at least two years. Girls were taught housekeeping skills at home. The city-state of Corinth was famous for its bronze statues, pottery, and vase painters. For a long time, the city was a leader in literature and the arts. The style of architecture we call Corinthian developed here. The Corinthians were also creative problem-solvers. To solve the problem of foreign money pouring into the *polis*, they created their own coinage and forced traders to convert their coins at Corinthian banks. To solve the problem of unemployment, they created a huge public-works program. Literature, culture, art, and business all flourished in Corinth. In the event of a conflict, they were more likely to support Argos and Megara than Athens and Sparta.

Argos

The city-state of Argos was located on a plain near Corinth. The weather was hot and dry in the summer, and cold and wet in the winter. Since the soil was not very fertile and the climate was extreme, growing food was a struggle. The arts were well developed in Argos. The sculptors of Argos created magnificent statues of athletes. There were many fine Argive musicians and poets. And the theater of Argos was excellent, drawing crowds of up to 20,000. Unfortunately, Argos made a serious mistake after the battle of Thermopylae in 480 B.C. When Athens and Sparta asked the *polis* to send supplies and troops to fight the Persians, Argos refused. The other Greek city-states held Argos in contempt after that. Argos was more likely to support Corinth or Megara than Athens or Sparta.

Megara

The city-state of Megara lay on the coast near Corinth. Schooling in Megara was similar to schooling in Athens or Corinth. Students memorized poetry and studied drama, public speaking, writing, science, the flute, and the lyre. They also learned a great deal of mathematics. Megara had its own coinage, and was famous for its wonderful textiles. Megara founded colonies in the Mediterranean, including the city that later became Byzantium, then Constantinople, then Istanbul. Given a choice, Megara would support Argos or Corinth rather than Sparta or Athens. But if forced to choose between Sparta and Athens, then Megara would support Sparta.

(continued)

The City-States of Greece *(continued)*

1. Because of the mountainous terrain, it was hard to travel by land from one Greek city-state to another. It was much easier to go by boat—but even that was dangerous. Locate Sparta, Athens, Corinth, Argos, and Megara on the map of ancient Greece below. What routes are possible from one city to another?

2. Use a topographic map of modern Greece and the information on this hand-out to create a board game based on Greek city-states. Show each city-state, and the possible routes from that city to the others. Include as many impor-tant features of each city-state as you can. Then set up hazards and rewards along the routes. You should make a full-size game board and any other mate-rials, like cards or trading goods, that you will need to play the game.

3. Create a full set of rules for playing your game. Write them out as clearly as you can.

4. When all groups have completed their games, follow your teacher's directions to try one another's games.

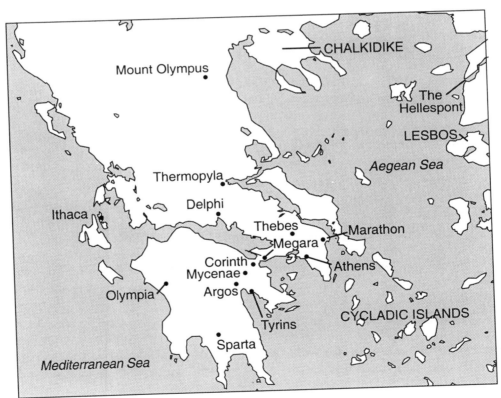

Map of ancient Greece

The Beginnings of Democracy

OBJECTIVES

Social Studies

- Students will be able to define Athenian democracy.
- Students will learn about early forms of government in Greece.
- Students will understand the concept of citizenship in ancient Greece.
- Students will understand the structure of the world's first democracy.
- Students will understand the function of ostracism in Athenian democracy.

MATERIALS

The Beginnings of Democracy handout
torn pieces of cardboard or oaktag
black or terra-cotta tempera
paper clips or other sharp utensils

BACKGROUND

The earliest democratic government arose in Athens around the year 508 B.C. The city-state of Athens covered an area of about 1,000 square miles (2,590 sq km), with a population of about 300,000. Of these, about 45,000 people were citizens and had the right to vote. These citizens were organized into a number of small communities called *demes*. These demes were combined to form larger groups called *trittyes*. There were 30 trittyes in all: 10 from the coast, 10 from the city, and 10 from the country. In turn the trittyes formed part of larger groups called the *phylae*, or tribes. There were 10 tribes, each made up of three trittyes. But while the trittyes were made up of people from the same area, the tribes were not. Each tribe included one trittys each from the city, the country, and the coast.

The laws of Athens were made by the Assembly, or *ecclesia*. This consisted of any citizens of Athens who chose to take part. The Assembly met about every 10 days at the Pnyx, a hill in Athens.

To take care of the day-to-day business of the city, a council was chosen each year. The members of this council—called the *bouleterion*—were chosen by lot. Fifty citizens were chosen from each tribe. The entire bouleterion consisted of 500 citizens. The bouleterion drew up policies and laws to present to the Assembly.

After the bouleterion presented its policies to the Assembly, the Assembly discussed them and voted on them. All citizens had the right to say what they thought before the Assembly and to vote on proposals made to the Assembly. If the majority of the Assembly voted in favor of a proposal, that proposal became law.

The generals, or *strategoi*, of Athens could be seen as the city-state's chief executive officers. The bouleterion suggested policies, and the ecclesia voted on them. The strategoi were the ones who put these policies into effect. There were

10 generals, one from each tribe of Athens, and they were elected annually. However, the same person could be reelected general a number of times.

Since all citizens were—or could be—members of the ecclesia, and the 500 members of the bouleterion could serve for one year only, there was small risk in the council that one man would take too much power. The risk lay with the strategoi, who could hold their positions for years. As a safeguard against this, a vote was held once a year at which any citizen could write one name on an *ostrakon*, a bit of broken pottery. If 6,000 citizens wrote the same man's name, that man was exiled—ostracized—from Athens for 10 years. The annual vote on ostracism was used only 10 times in the 90 years that it was legal, and several times the man who had been ostracized was recalled within a few years to serve the city. The exile was the only penalty of ostracism; lands and property were not confiscated.

A story is told about Aristides the Just, a hero of the Battle of Marathon. At the ostracism vote of 482 B.C. an illiterate farmer, who didn't know Aristides, approached him and asked him to write the name "Aristides" on an ostrakon, as he could not write it himself. Aristides asked the farmer, "What harm has Aristides ever done you?" The farmer replied, "None at all, nor do I know him. I am just tired of hearing everyone call him 'the Just.'" Aristides complied, and wrote his own name on the ostrakon. When the votes were counted, Aristides was ostracized. (He was recalled to deal with a crisis two years later.)

PROCEDURE

1. Distribute the handout, and discuss the Athenian democratic structure. Have students brainstorm the strengths and weaknesses of such a structure.

2. Discuss current politics and politicians. Have students speculate on the effect on our government if one politician had to step out of politics for 10 years. Students then choose one person from their own country's history that they would like to have step down.

3. Direct students to prepare their own ostrakon for voting by painting pieces of cardboard black or terra cotta (the typical colors of Athenian pottery).

4. Have students use a paper clip or other tool to scratch a name through the paint on the ostrakon.

5. Appoint three or four students to collect and tally the votes. Did any one name lead the voting for ostracism?

VARIATION

If students have already done the Greek alphabet activity on page 15, encourage them to use the Greek alphabet to write the name on their ostrakon.

Ριχηαρδ M. Νιξον (Richard M. Nixon)

Βενεδιχτ Αρνολδ (Benedict Arnold)

The Beginnings of Democracy

Each city-state in Greece had its own characteristics. Different cities developed different types of government. For a long time, most Greek states were ruled by groups of rich landowners. Gradually, other people began to want a say in decision making. In some places, riots broke out. To restore peace, people in some city-states agreed to let one man have complete control. These leaders were called *tyrants*. When tyrants fell from power, civil war often followed.

Around 508 B.C. an Athenian named Cleisthenes had an idea for stopping the cycle of tyrant, rebellion, and civil war. He suggested a whole new system of government. This new system would involve a lot more people in governing the city. The Greek word for people was *demos*, and the word for government was *kratos*. These words were eventually combined to give a name to the new system: *demokratia*—democracy.

This new system involved all the citizens of Athens in government. However, it's important to remember that the term "citizens of Athens" wasn't the same as "people of Athens." Citizenship was open only to free adult men whose parents were Athenian. Women, slaves, and foreigners were not eligible for citizenship. In 451 B.C. the population of Athens was about 300,000. This included about 75,000

A vote of ostracism

slaves, 35,000 foreigners, 100,000 children of citizens, and 35,000 wives of citizens. Only 45,000—15 percent—of the people who lived in Athens were actually citizens and eligible to vote.

The laws of Athens were made by the Assembly, or *ecclesia*. This consisted of any citizens of Athens who chose to take part. The Assembly met about every 10 days at the Pnyx, a hill in Athens. At least 6,000 citizens had to be present to hold a meeting of the Assembly. If too few citizens came, special police were sent out to bring more citizens to the meeting. These meetings began early in the morning and could go on until dark. The Assembly decided on laws and public policies like taxes and building programs.

To take care of the day-to-day business of the city, a council called the *bouleterion* was chosen each year. The council consisted of 500 citizens, 50 from each of the 10 tribes of Athens. They were chosen by lot by having their names drawn from a container. The council drew up policies and laws to present to the Assembly.

(continued)

Hands-on Culture of Ancient Greece and Rome

The Beginnings of Democracy (continued)

The Athenian democracy also included a board of 10 generals, the *strategoi*. These generals were elected, not chosen by lot. One was chosen from each tribe. The generals were more than military leaders. They were the ones who carried out the decisions of the council and the Assembly. They met with foreign envoys to Athens, and supervised state officials like tax collectors and ship repairers. There was no time limit on serving as general. The same person could be reelected general many times.

To make sure that no one person could become too powerful, the Athenian democratic system included one more safeguard. Once a year a special vote was held in the Assembly. Bits of broken pottery called *ostrakon* were used as ballots. Any citizen present at the meeting could choose the man he most wanted to have leave Athens, and write that man's name on an ostrakon. If 6,000 or more citizens named one person, that man had to leave Athens for 10 years. No charges had to be made against him, much less proven; he just had to leave. (This is the source of the English word *ostracism*.)

Imagine that our democratic system included ostracism. How would it affect politics?

1. Think about people who are active in politics today. This can be at any level: local, state, or national. Do you think things would improve if one of these people had to leave politics for 10 years? Choose one name to write on an ostrakon.

2. Prepare an ostrakon for the vote. The Athenians used broken pottery because there was always plenty of it available. You will use a piece of cardboard or oaktag as your ostrakon. Paint it black or terra cotta. These were the typical colors of Athenian pottery.

3. Use a paper clip or other sharp tool to scratch a name in the paint of your ostrakon.

Ostrakon naming Kimon of Athens, ostracized in 461 B.C.

Trials and Time

OBJECTIVES

Social Studies
- Students will learn about the Athenian development of the trial by jury.
- Students will learn how people in the ancient world kept track of time.

Science
- Students will understand how ancient peoples used available technology.

Art
- Students will create a *clepsydra*, or Greek water clock.

MATERIALS

Trials and Time handout
<u>For each group:</u>

two plastic bowls	masking tape
permanent marker	measuring cup
box (or other support) that is taller than the height of the bowls	hammer and nail
	stopwatch or clock with second hand

BACKGROUND

The concept of trial by jury is one of ancient Greece's greatest legacies. The Athenian jury was a committee of people appointed to listen to both sides at a trial. Once the jury had given a decision, it could not be appealed; the decision was final. Each jury consisted of more than 200 men to ensure against intimidation and bribery. After 461 B.C., jurors were paid to compensate for loss of earnings. This meant that all citizens, rich and poor, could afford to be in the jury pool.

PROCEDURE

1. Distribute the handout. Divide students into groups of three or four. Students proceed as directed to build a water clock.
2. When all groups have completed their water clocks and have calibrated them individually, have groups compare their calibrations to see if all the water clocks are calibrated in the same way. Encourage student discussion of the limitations of this kind of timekeeper.

EXTENSION

Have students use the water clock to determine ounces, cups, and inches of time. How many minutes are shown by one inch on the water clock? If people still used water clocks, might we say "I'll be there in three inches"? Why or why not?

Trials and Time

Beginning with the earliest civilizations, people have developed systems of laws. If it could be proved that someone had broken the law, he or she would be punished. In most early legal systems, a person accused of a crime was brought before a judge. The judge decided whether the person was guilty.

The Athenians developed a new system: **trial by jury**. In this system, any citizen who was accused of a crime was allowed to present his version of events to a group of other citizens. This group was the jury.

The jury system was based on a pool of volunteer jurors. Every year, all citizens over 30 were expected to volunteer for jury service. From then on, all names were chosen by lot. First, a panel of 6,000 jurors was chosen from all the volunteers. Each citizen selected as a juror was given a ticket with his name on it. If a juror actually served during a trial, he handed in his ticket when he entered the court. At the end of the trial, he was given back his ticket and was paid for his work as a juror.

For each trial, all jurors who were available and interested came to the court. A jury of at least 201 citizens was chosen. As each juror entered the court, he handed over his juror ticket and was given two bronze tokens. One of these tokens had a hole in the middle and one didn't. When the time came for the jury to vote, each juror chose one token. The token with the raised center meant a vote of innocent. The one

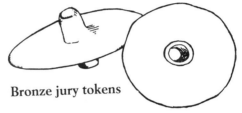

Bronze jury tokens

with the hollow center meant a vote of guilty. Each juror covered the center of the token with his finger, so that no one could see how he was voting, and dropped the token into an urn. The votes were counted. If most of the tokens were solid, the accused was pronounced innocent. If most of them were hollow, he was found guilty.

Some jurors were chosen to do certain tasks. One was named judge. One was appointed to count the votes at the end. And a third was put in charge of the water clock.

Then the trial could begin. The Athenian system had no professional judges, lawyers, or legal officials. The person on trial had to speak for himself. Some people hired speechwriters to prepare their speeches, but only the accused could present the speech in court.

The length of each speech was controlled by a *clepsydra*, or water clock. One juror watched the clock. A certain amount of time was allowed for each speech. When that time ran out, the speaker had to stop.

**Clepsydra
(Greek water clock)**

(continued)

Trials and Time *(continued)*

These clocks were very different from the clocks we use today. Essentially, they consisted of two jars. One jar had a hole in it near the base. This jar was put on a stand so that it was higher than the other jar. Then the top jar was filled with water. The water would run out through the hole and fall into the lower jar. This worked like an hourglass or egg timer filled with sand. The water flowed out of the upper jar at a constant rate. If you always put in the same amount of water, it would always take the same amount of time to flow out. So it could be used like an egg timer, to set a certain length of time.

A water clock could also be calibrated. Marks could be made on the jar to show divisions of time. If you knew that it took six hours for the upper jar to empty, you could mark six levels on it, one for each hour. Then you could tell how much time had passed by checking the level of water in the jar.

1. You can use two plastic bowls to make your own water clock. Use a hammer and a thin nail to make a small hole near the bottom of one of the bowls.

2. Place the bowl with the hole on a stand so that it is above the other bowl.

3. Pour water into the upper bowl. It will flow into the lower bowl.

4. To calibrate your water clock, put a strip of masking tape on the side of the lower jar. One partner should look at a clock with a second hand while the other marks the time on the masking tape with a permanent marker. Begin timing when the second hand is on the 12. When it reaches the 12 again, the clock watcher should say "one." The other partner should make a mark on the masking tape to show the level of water in the lower bowl after one minute. Repeat for two minutes, three minutes, etc.

Alpha, Beta, Alphabet

OBJECTIVES

Social Studies
- Students will become familiar with the letters of the classical Greek alphabet.
- Students will convert Greek letters to their Roman counterparts.
- Students will convert Roman letters to their Greek counterparts.

English/Language Arts
- Students will understand the history of the development of the alphabet.

Math/Science
- Students will understand the origin of some terms and symbols used in writing math and science.

MATERIALS

Alpha, Beta, Alphabet handout
writing materials

BACKGROUND

Before the Phoenicians developed their alphabet in the twelfth century B.C., other cultures had developed writing systems that were at least partially alphabetic. However, none of these systems appear to have fully developed this concept. The Phoenician 22-letter system was completely alphabetic. It was the direct ancestor of the alphabet we use today.

When the Greeks adopted the Phoenician system, they modified it. Some of these modifications may have been unintentional. It is often hard to distinguish slight differences in a foreign language's sounds. For example, most English speakers can't distinguish the sounds of the French words "roux" (reddish) and "rue" (street). It is easy to imagine an eager Greek some 3,000 years ago trying to imitate the sounds of a Phoenician trader as the Phoenician explained the alphabet. Perhaps this is how the Phoenician *aleph, beth, gimel* became *alpha, beta, gamma*. Perhaps this is also how letters for vowels were introduced into the alphabet. Some Phoenician consonants were weak sounds; the Greek vowel sounds may have been the closest a Greek adapter could come to them.

The early Greek alphabet was very close in appearance to the Phoenician one. Over time, the classical Greek alphabet—known as the Ionian alphabet—developed from this early alphabet.

However, long before the Ionian alphabet developed, the Greeks had started colonizing other parts of the Mediterranean. Colonists to Italy had brought the earlier alphabet with them. This alphabet was adopted—and further modified—by the Etruscans, and then by the Romans. It eventually became the Roman alphabet we use today.

PROCEDURE

1. Distribute the handout. Ask students if any of the Greek symbols or letter names are familiar to them. The names alpha and beta, as components of our word alphabet, may be recognized, as may the symbol and word π (*pi*), which is the name of a mathematical ratio.

2. Model for students the process of writing Greek words using Greek letters, then Roman letters. As students work through this part of the activity, they may be surprised to discover some familiar words. Students should realize that the unfamiliar symbols constitute a bigger barrier to understanding than do the actual Greek words.

3. Model writing an English word or sentence with Greek letters. Students will need to sound out the English letters to choose the most appropriate Greek letter. On a separate sheet of paper, students should write a simple sentence using Greek letters.

4. When all students have completed their sentences, divide the class into pairs. Partners exchange sentences and try to read the sentence each has been given.

ANSWERS

α ρ ο μ α	aroma
α σ θ μ α	asthma
δ ι λ ε μ μ α	dilemma
δ ι π λ ο μ α	diploma
δ ρ α μ α	drama
κ ι ν ε μ α	kinema (cinema)
κ ο μ μ α	comma
π ρ ο β λ ε μ α	problema (problem)

Bonus answer: Many of these symbols are used in writing mathematics.

EXTENSION

Have students practice using Greek letters with other activities in this book. The Greek spellings of many Greek words are included in the glossary.

Alpha, Beta, Alphabet

When you learned to read and write in English, you started by learning the alphabet. Did you ever wonder where that alphabet came from?

An **alphabet** is a writing system that uses one symbol for each sound in the language. The symbols can be combined to represent different words. The world's earliest writing systems didn't use this system. Some of them used a different symbol for each word. Some of them used a symbol for each syllable. Then, around 1100 B.C., the Phoenicians, a seafaring people in the Mediterranean, developed a different approach. They came up with 22 symbols for individual sounds: the first alphabet.

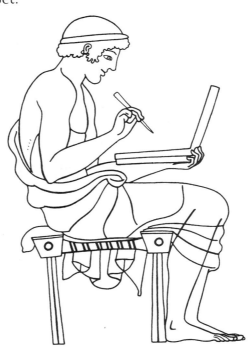

A Greek scribe

The Phoenicians traded all around the Mediterranean. Contact with the Greeks was bound to come. At some point—historians aren't sure when—the Greeks started to use the Phoenician alphabet. They also changed it. The 22 symbols of the Phoenician alphabet were all consonants; there were no symbols for vowels. Readers had to figure out what the vowel sounds should be. Somehow, as the Greeks adopted the alphabet, some of the sounds changed from consonants to vowels, and some new signs were added. The names for the letters changed, too. The first two sounds in the Phoenician alphabet had been *aleph* and *beth*. In Greek they became *alpha* and *beta*—which eventually led to our word "alphabet."

Here are the letters of the classical Greek alphabet, with their names and the closest corresponding English sound.

(continued)

Alpha, Beta, Alphabet (continued)

Capital Letter	Small Letter	Name	Sound in English
A	α	alpha	a
B	β	beta	b
Γ	γ	gamma	g
Δ	δ	delta	d
E	ε	epsilon	e (as in "get")
Z	ζ	zeta	z, sd (as in "wisdom")
H	η	eta	e (as in "hair")
Θ	θ	theta	th (as in "think")
I	ι	iota	i (as in "peep")
K	κ	kappa	k, c (as in "cat")
Λ	λ	lambda	l
M	μ	mu	m
N	ν	nu	n
Ξ	ξ	xi	x, ks
O	o	omicron	o (as in "pot")
Π	π	pi	p
P	ρ	rho	r
Σ	σ, ς*	sigma	s *(written ς when last letter of word)
T	τ	tau	t
Υ	υ	upsilon	u, y
Φ	φ	phi	ph, f
X	χ	chi	kh
Ψ	ψ	psi	ps
Ω	ω	omega	o (as in "paw")

Although our alphabet developed from the Greek alphabet, some of their symbols are confusing. The symbol for **rho**, the Greek "r" sound, is ρ—it looks like our symbol for "p." The symbol for **omega**, the long "o" sound, is ω—it looks like our "w." And some Greek symbols, like ψ and φ, don't look like any of our letters.

Also, the Greeks didn't have a separate symbol for the "h" sound. Instead, they made a mark like an apostrophe before a vowel to show the "h." So the word Ἑρμες would be pronounced "Hermes."

(continued)

Hands-on Culture of Ancient Greece and Rome

Alpha, Beta, Alphabet *(continued)*

Practice writing the Greek symbols. Here are a few Greek words. Try copying them using the Greek letters. Then write them out using the closest English letters. Do these words look familiar to you now?

α ρ ο μ α _____ _____

α σ θ μ α _____ _____

δ ι λ ε μ μ α _____ _____

δ ι π λ ο μ α _____ _____

δ ρ α μ α _____ _____

κ ι ν ε μ α _____ _____

κ ο μ μ α _____ _____

π ρ ο β λ ε μ α _____ _____

Even though some of the symbols are very different, Greek letters can be used to write most of the sounds in English. Some English letters are missing from the Greek alphabet. Use these Greek letters instead.

For j, use ι

For c, use κ or σ (depending on whether the sound should be hard or soft)

For v, use φ

For w, use ου

For y, use ι or ευ

<u>Example:</u> We walked to school today.

Ουι ουαλκδ τυ σκυλ τεδη.

Prepare a simple English sentence. Now use Greek symbols to write out the words. Write the Greek sentence neatly on a separate piece of paper. Then exchange sentences with a partner. Can you read your partner's sentence?

_____

_____

Bonus: Many Greek symbols are still used in one area of knowledge today. Which area is that?

It's Greek to Me

OBJECTIVES

Social Studies

- Students will learn about some effects of Greek culture on ours.

English/Language Arts

- Students will learn some common Greek roots.
- Students will identify English words based on Greek roots.
- Students will be able to use Greek roots to guess at the meaning of unfamiliar words.

MATERIALS

It's Greek to Me handout
good dictionary that provides etymologies

BACKGROUND

Although English belongs to the Germanic language family, it owes a large debt to Greek. As many as one sixth of the words in the English language are of Greek origin. *Theater* and *drama*, *planet* and *astronomy*, *metropolis* and *monarch*— all these words are based on Greek.

PROCEDURE

1. Begin by telling students that they already know a lot of Greek words, even if they don't realize it. Explain that the words *bicycle, geometry,* and *alphabet,* among others, come from Greek. Distribute the handout.

2. Go through the list of Greek word roots. Model combining the root words to form two or three common English words.

3. Students work individually or in groups to list as many English words as possible that are made using the Greek roots.

4. Once students have completed their lists, have them look up the words in a dictionary. Some students will have included word they have heard of but whose meanings they don't know. Some may have combined Greek word roots to make plausible-sounding, but non-existent, words—e.g., *megaphobe, autohydro.*

ANSWERS

These roots can be combined in many different ways, including:

anthropology
antithesis
astrology
autograph
biology
democracy
demographic
geography
geology

geometry
graph
graphology
hydrophobia
megaphone
meter
microbiology
micrograph
micrometer

microphone
microscope
phonogram
phonology
polygraph
polyphony
symmetry
telescope
telegraph

VARIATION

This activity can also be done as a game. Prepare laminated cards of each Greek root word on the handout. Divide class into groups, and give each group a set of laminated cards. Groups work together to brainstorm English words based on the Greek roots. To play, groups take turns. One group member holds up one or more cards with Greek roots to form one English word, then defines the word. If no other group has that word on their list, the team receives one point. If another group has the word, both groups strike out the word and no points are received. The winning team is the one that has the most points at the end of the game.

EXTENSION

Here are some useful Greek word roots:

cosmo—world (microcosm)
chrom—color (monochrome)
chron—time (chronometer)
cycle—circle (bicycle)
dynami—power, force (dynamic)
hypo—under (hypodermic)
meta—beyond (metaphysics)
mono—one, alone (monocle)
onym—name, word (synonym)

pan—all (pantheism)
path—feeling (sympathy)
peri—around (perimeter)
phil—love (Anglophile)
phob—fear (hydrophobia)
pseudo—false (pseudonym)
psych—mind (psychology)
theo—god (theology)
therm—heat (thermal)

It's Greek to Me

Have you ever heard the saying, "It's Greek to me"? People use it when they can't make sense out of something. But, most English speakers actually know quite a lot of Greek.

The reason for this goes back a long way—to the sixth century B.C. At that time, Greek scientists and thinkers were making great advances. Greek scientists and geographers believed that the earth was round. They even estimated what its circumference might be. Greek astronomers studied the movements of the stars and named many constellations. They knew that the moon did not produce light, but reflected the light of the sun. Greek mathematicians worked out many basic rules of mathematics. They developed theorems in geometry that are still used today. Greek thinkers wrote about many of their ideas, including ideas about philosophy and government.

The Greek words for many of these concepts—like life, self, human, and water—ended up as part of the English language. In fact, the Greeks had words for many key concepts. These words could be combined to form new words. As long as people knew the meanings of the Greek words, they could figure out the meanings of the new words.

To make this word-forming process easier, people didn't always use the whole word. They just used the essential part of the word. This is called the **word root**. For example, the Greek word for "small" is *micros*. The word root is *micro*. The Greek word for "look" is *scopeo*. The word root is *scop*. The two roots can be combined to make a word for something that looks at small things—*microscope*.

Here are some common Greek word roots, with their English meanings. Think of as many English words as you can that are made with these Greek words. Write a list of the English words and the Greek words that they use. When your list is finished, look up the meanings of five of the words in the dictionary. If you had known the meaning of the Greek words, could you have guessed at the meaning of the English ones?

Greek word roots and their English meanings		
anti—against	*anthropo*—human	*astro*—star
auto—self	*bio*—life	*cracy*—government
dem—people	*geo*—earth	*graph*—draw, write
hydro—water	*macro*—large	*mega*—big
meter—measure	*micro*—small	*mono*—single, alone
logy—study, science	*phob*—fear	*phon*—sound
poly—many	*scop*—see, look at	*syn, sym*—together
tele—far	*thesis*—proposition	

Greek Gods and Goddesses

OBJECTIVES

Social Studies

- Students will analyze the important attributes of the Greek gods to make deductions about Greek culture.

English/Language Arts

- Students will become familiar with the major gods of the Greek pantheon.

Art

- Students will create an illustration of a Greek god or goddess.

MATERIALS

Greek Gods and Goddesses handout
paper or poster board
art supplies
optional: slides or photos showing Greek representations of the gods

BACKGROUND

Although some Greeks scoffed at the idea of a panoply of gods deciding on the fates of humans from their home on Mount Olympus, many more believed in the gods and their powers. The common people of Greece often suffered at the hands of the wealthy; they called on the gods for help.

Many Greeks also believed that the gods would give them information about hidden things, including the future. The oracle at Delphi was supposed to speak for Apollo. At other shrines, tablets have been found with questions to put to the gods: "Gerioton asks Zeus whether he should marry," or "Did Dorcilus steal the cloth?"

The Greek pantheon included many gods besides the ones described on the student handout. Here is a partial listing:

Asclepius—son of Apollo, the god of medicine

Dionysus—son of Zeus and Semele, god of wine and pleasure

Fates—the three daughters of night; they spun out the thread of each human's destiny, then cut the thread when the person was fated to die.

Furies—three goddesses of vengeance; they punished those who committed serious crimes.

Hestia—sister of Zeus, goddess of the hearth, protectress of house, family, and city

Hygea—daughter of Asclepius, the goddess of health

Muses—the nine daughters of Zeus and Mnemosyne (Memory); each protected a different area of science, literature, and the arts.

Persephone—daughter of Zeus and Demeter, wife of Hades, queen of the underworld

PROCEDURE

1. This activity can be done as a group activity, with two or three students working on each poster.

2. Distribute the handout, and discuss the Greek pantheon. If you wish, show slides or photographs of Greek statues and vase paintings that show Greek deities.

3. Have students read the descriptions of the gods. Based on the area each god protected or governed, what do these descriptions tell students about Greek life? What was important to the Greeks?

4. Students choose one of the gods and goddesses on the handout, and proceed as directed. Mount the completed posters in the classroom.

EXTENSION

Have each student research myths associated with the chosen god or goddess. The student should write a brief summary of a myth at the foot of the poster, or illustrate a scene from the myth.

VARIATIONS

- Have students prepare a family tree for the gods.
- The Romans adopted many Greek gods. The Roman gods had the same attributes and characteristics as the Greek gods, but had different names.

Greek	Roman	Greek	Roman
Aphrodite	— Venus	Hades	— Pluto
Apollo	— Apollo	Hephaestus	— Vulcan
Ares	— Mars	Hermes	— Mercury
Artemis	— Diana	Hestia	— Vesta
Athena	— Minerva	Poseidon	— Neptune
Demeter	— Ceres	Zeus	— Jupiter
Dionysus	— Bacchus		

Have students do the activity using the Roman names for the gods.

Greek Gods and Goddesses

Early people knew nothing about the laws of nature, but they were aware of nature itself. They heard the echo effect in the mountains. They saw how the seasons changed during the year. Like many other early people, the Greeks tried to find explanations for the things they found in nature. They came to believe that divine beings oversaw what went on in the world. These gods and goddesses had great powers. They lived forever on top of a mountain, Mount Olympus. And, in many ways, these gods were very like the humans who believed in them. They were born, they fell in love, they married and had children. Sometimes they were angry, or mischievous, or dishonest. Legends arose to describe the gods' personalities to teach people what would please or anger the gods.

These are some of the most important Greek deities.

Aphrodite *(af-ro-DI-te)*

The daughter of Zeus and Dione, she was the goddess of love and beauty. Born in the sea, she rode to shore in a scallop shell, surrounded by dolphins. Although she married Hephaestus, she loved Ares, his brother.

Apollo *(a-POL-lo)*

The son of Zeus and Leto, he was god of the sun, archery, music, medicine, and prophecy. He protected the herds and young men. He was usually shown with a lyre, a bow and arrows, or a shepherd's crooked stick.

Ares *(A-reez)*

A son of Zeus and Hera, Ares was the god of aggressive war. Short-tempered and violent, he was often shown with a spear and war helmet.

Artemis *(AR-te-mis)*

Daughter of Zeus, twin sister of Apollo, she was the goddess of the moon, wild animals, and hunting. She protected maidens, and women giving birth. She was usually shown carrying a bow and arrows, accompanied by a dog or a doe.

Athena *(a-THEE-na)*

The daughter of Zeus, Athena was the goddess of wisdom, defensive war, and the art of peace. She was also the patron goddess of Athens. Her symbols were the owl and the olive. She was usually shown with war helmet, spear, and shield.

Demeter *(de-MEET-er)*

Sister of Zeus, Demeter was the goddess of the earth, grain, and agriculture. She was usually shown crowned with a ribbon and carrying either a torch or a sheaf of wheat.

(continued)

Hands-on Culture of Ancient Greece and Rome

Greek Gods and Goddesses (continued)

Hades (HAY-deez)

Hades, one of Zeus's brothers, ruled the land of the dead. When the soul of a dead person arrived in the underworld, Hades sat in judgment to decide the soul's fate. Most souls were sent to Tartarus, the place of punishment. A few were sent to the home of the blessed, the Elysian Fields.

Hephaestus (he-FES-tus)

This son of Zeus and Hera was the divine blacksmith, the god of fire. He protected artisans whose crafts were related to his own, such as toolmakers, armorers, and potters. He married Aphrodite, but she was not faithful to him. He was often shown holding the tools of his trade: the bellows, hammer, and tongs.

Hera (HE-ra)

Hera was Zeus's sister and wife, the queen of the gods. She was the protector of children and married women, but her own husband, Zeus, was constantly unfaithful. She is often shown holding a scepter. On top of the scepter are a cuckoo and a pomegranate. The peacock, her favorite bird, was sacred to her.

Hermes (HER-meez)

Another son of Zeus, by Maia, Hermes was the god of trade, travelers, and thieves. He was also the messenger of the other gods. Hermes was usually shown wearing a round hat with wings, winged sandals, and a winged staff with serpents twisted around it.

Poseidon (poh-SAI-dun)

A brother of Zeus, he was given control over earthquakes and the sea. Poseidon was moody and violent. He raced over the waves in a chariot pulled by white horses, carrying a trident, or three-pointed spear. Poseidon was the protector of sailors, but he was also known to cause storms and shipwrecks when angry.

Zeus (Zoos)

Zeus was the ruler of all the gods. He was god of the sky and of heavenly phenomena like lightning, thunder, and rain. Zeus was often shown with a thunderbolt in his right hand, a scepter in his left hand, and an eagle at his feet.

Choose one of the gods or goddesses described on these pages. Make a poster showing this deity with the symbols he or she usually carried.

Greek Myths

OBJECTIVES

Social Studies

- Students will see how early people used myths to explain natural phenomena.
- Students will recognize that they can learn about a culture from its myths.

English/Language Arts

- Students will create their own myths to explain a natural phenomenon.

MATERIALS

Greek Myths handout
writing materials
optional: other explanation myths

BACKGROUND

Myths from all cultures include stories that explain natural phenomena, reflecting a human need to find some order in apparent chaos. Reading myths can help us understand what people thought long ago, what they knew, what they feared.

PROCEDURE

1. This activity works best as a group activity, with two or three students working on each myth.

2. Distribute the handout, and discuss the concept of explanation stories. If you wish, share other explanation myths with students.

3. Have students brainstorm a list of things in nature that seem to call for explanation. Items on the list should be in the form of questions, e.g., Why is the sky blue? Where do thunder and lightning come from? What causes mirages on the road on sunny days? Why do mosquitoes buzz in your ear before they bite?

4. Have each group (or each individual student, if you prefer) choose a question, then develop a myth to answer the question.

5. When all stories are completed, students should present their stories orally to the class. Make copies of all stories for a classroom mythology anthology.

VARIATION

Have students research Greek myths of explanation, then choose one myth and illustrate at least four scenes from the myth. Display the illustrations in groups in the classroom.

Name _____ Date _____

Greek Myths

If you didn't understand the seasons of the year, how would you explain them? The Greeks used myths to answer questions about life and nature. This myth, the story of Persephone, was used to explain the different seasons of the year.

Long ago, when the gods were young, Demeter, goddess of the harvest, made her home on the earth. Every day she walked out across the fields. Where she walked, the fruit ripened on the trees and the grain grew full in the fields. And in the evening Demeter came home to her daughter, Persephone. As the world was filled with joy by Demeter, Demeter was filled with joy by Persephone.

Demeter, goddess of the harvest

But one day Hades, lord of the underworld, noticed Persephone. He felt that her sunny nature would bring light to the dark underworld. He stole Persephone away and tried to convince her to marry him.

On earth, Demeter was miserable without her daughter. She no longer walked the fields, bringing sunshine and ripeness. Instead, she wept for her daughter. And as Demeter wept, the earth wept. Rain fell. The land grew cold. The crops no longer grew in the fields. The people prayed to Zeus to help them, or they would starve.

Zeus ordered Hades to let Persephone return to earth. But Hades loved Persephone too much to see her leave. He tricked her into eating six pomegranate seeds. Since Persephone had eaten the food of the dead, she was now bound to the underworld. For six months every year, Persephone returns to Hades. Then Demeter mourns, and the earth grows dark and cold. When Persephone returns to the world above, Demeter smiles again, and the earth brings forth its riches.

The story of Demeter, Persephone, and Hades reflects the Greek culture that created it. Create your own explanation myth, reflecting your life and culture. Your myth could explain the origin of the seasons, like this Greek myth, or it could explain some other aspect of nature. Illustrate your story, if you wish.

Tragedy and Comedy

OBJECTIVES

Social Studies

- Students will understand the history and development of Greek theater.
- Students will identify and critique an issue or concern in their world.

English

- Students will be able to define tragedy and comedy.
- Students will create a play using satire and caricature.

Art

- Students will design and create masks.

MATERIALS

Tragedy and Comedy handout
art supplies for making masks
optional: newspaper or newsmagazine photographs and caricatures of
   public figures

BACKGROUND

The Greek theater tradition developed out of Greek religion. Tragedy evolved from sacrifices to the god Dionysus. Perhaps at some point goats were the sacrifice; the word *tragedy* means "goat cry." In Greek tragedy, the figures in a play are sacrificed to an implacable deity. Plays deal with kingly heroes destroyed by divine command. Since most plays were based on Greek myths, with which the audience was already familiar, the suspense in Greek theater was not "what will happen next?" but "how will it happen?" The great playwrights of ancient Greece—Aeschylus, Sophocles, and Euripides, for example—retold the familiar stories in their own way, stressing some parts of the story and leaving out others as it suited them.

Comedy also developed from a religious base, but a very different one. Its origin was in rustic fertility rites, wild and obscene. Both wildness and obscenity remained a feature of Greek comedy.

Greek theater was an integral part of the community. On certain traditional dates, festivals were held in honor of the gods. All work stopped for the duration of the festival. After the time of Pericles, working people in Athens were paid to take time off work and attend the theater. Tragedies, comedies, and satyr plays were all produced on the same day, on the same stage. The best plays were awarded a prize.

PROCEDURE

1. Distribute the handout and discuss the idea of social comment. Brainstorm some of the kinds of things students might want to comment on. The issues could be global or local, from damage to the ozone layer to a town's refusal to build a bike lane on a scenic road.

2. Explain to students the concepts of satire and caricature. Satire uses devices like irony, sarcasm, and ridicule to expose folly and vice. A caricature is a representation, either in words or images, where the peculiarities of a person or thing are exaggerated, but a general likeness is maintained. Political cartoons often use caricature. If you wish, show students photographs and caricatures of political figures to help them see how artists use exaggeration to make a point.

3. Divide students into groups of four or five. Each group is to decide on a topic for a play. Direct students to develop and write their plays using one or two actors and a chorus. Each play should be 5 to 10 minutes long.

4. Distribute mask-making materials. The masks can be as simple as stick masks or as complex as papier-mâché, depending on time and materials available. (To make a stick mask, students cut a large mask shape from stiff paper, with holes for the eyes and mouth, and attach it to a short stick. The mask is held in front of the actor's face.) Students should create masks for both actors and chorus in their plays.

5. Student groups present their plays to the class.

EXTENSION

Have students present their finished plays to a wider audience.

An ancient dance

Tragedy and Comedy

How many movies have you seen in the past month? Did any of them seem to make fun of politics, or something else in our society? Or did a movie seem to tell the story of people destroyed by forces beyond their control? If you answered yes to either question, then the movie you saw was based on the tradition of Greek theater.

Greek theater had its roots in religious rites. Tragedy probably developed from ceremonies of sacrifice to the gods. Tragedies tell of people whose lives seem to be sacrificed to the gods, no matter how they try to avoid their fates.

Comedy, on the other hand, probably came from early fertility rites. The *komos* was a revel held for the god Dionysus. People dressed up as animals and weird creatures. As they danced and sang, they sometimes used the anonymity of their disguises to complain about problems, or about their leaders. As comedy developed, it kept the strange costumes. It also became a way to point out problems by making fun of them. Commenting on problems in this way is called *satire*. It is still used in plays and books today, and in things like political cartoons.

Tragedies and comedies were both produced in the same way. All the actors were men. In front of the stage, a group of 12 to 15 actors formed a chorus. They chanted songs or told the background to the story. On the stage itself, two or three actors presented the most dramatic events in the play. Because Greek theaters were so big—some held close to 20,000 people—the actors were far away from some of the audience. Actors wore stylized masks that were larger than life-size so people near the back could see them. To help even more with recognition, a certain style of mask was used to show different character types. One style of mask showed that the character was a king. Another style showed that the character was a messenger. The shape of the masks amplified the actors' voices so that they carried all the way to the back rows.

Greek theater mask

(continued)

Tragedy and Comedy (continued)

In Athens, plays were part of two important religious festivals. The celebrations included contests for the best tragedy and the best comedy. The tragedies told stories from Greek myths. Comedies told many different stories, and writers often used them to make political statements. Aristophanes, Athens' finest comedy writer, used his plays to comment on the leaders of Athens and on the war with Sparta. In *The Wasps* he presented one leader, Cleon, as a greedy man who used the citizens of Athens for his own purposes.

1. If you were going to use a play to comment on something in society, what would it be? Work in your group to decide on something you think is being handled badly by the people in charge. It could be something in your school, your community, the country, or the whole world.

2. Once you have chosen a topic, write a play that says exactly what you think is wrong. Your play should be about five minutes long. Use the Greek comic tradition of ridicule to make a point. Feel free to exaggerate. Think how political cartoonists work. They often pick some part of a person's appearance—say, a big nose, or dark eyebrows—then exaggerate that feature in a drawing. The exaggeration makes it funny, but it can also make the person easier to recognize. So use lots of exaggeration to make your point.

3. You will need one or two actors and a chorus for your play. The chorus will all read the same lines together. The actors will present a key dramatic scene.

4. Design and make masks for the actors and chorus.

5. Present your play to the class.

Potted History

OBJECTIVES

Social Studies

- Students will understand that the art of a culture can be a source of information about the culture.
- Students will become familiar with several common Greek pot shapes.
- Students will understand the uses of Greek pots.

Art

- Students will recognize, and be able to distinguish, Greek red-figured and black-figured ware.
- Students will paint a scene from their own lives in the style of Greek red-figured or black-figured ware.

MATERIALS

Potted History handout
art supplies, including black, terra-cotta, and white paint
slides or photos of Greek red-figured and black-figured pottery
optional: white and terra-cotta wax crayons

BACKGROUND

The earliest distinct style of Greek vase painting has been called Proto-Geometric. Painters decorated pots with concentric circles and semicircles, augmented with simple zigzags and wavy lines. By 900 B.C., this style had given way to the Geometric style. More patterns were used, including triangles and squares in alternating colors. By the eighth century B.C., animals were included in the designs; soon after that human figures began to appear, but they also were treated as a design motif.

The next style in Greek pottery is called the Orientalizing style. The angular geometric patterns of the earlier periods were softened. At the same time—around 700 B.C.—the black-figured technique was first introduced in Corinth. In this technique, *clay slip*—a thin mixture of clay and water—was used to paint figures and decorations on a natural clay ground. Details were scratched through the slip to expose the clay below. When fired, the painted area turned black, while the background of the pot changed to a terra-cotta color.

The black and red colors of the pots were created by a chemical reaction. As described above, part of the surface of the pot was coated in a watery clay slip, while the rest of the pot was left in its natural state. Then the pot was fired in a kiln. In the first stage of firing, the temperature in the kiln was raised to 800° C; the vents of the kiln were open to let in air. At that temperature, in the presence of air, both the plain clay and the slip turned red. Then the vents of the kiln were closed and the temperature was raised to 950° C. Again, both the slip and the clay reacted to the temperature and the lack of air, this time by turning black. The slip also had another reaction. It fused, so that air could no longer pass through it. In the third phase of firing, the air vents of the kiln were opened and the kiln was allowed to cool. As the air touched the pot, the exposed clay surface again turned red. But where the clay had been coated with slip, the surface was no longer exposed to the air; the coated areas stayed black.

Around 530 B.C. another new technique, red-figured painting, was introduced. In red-figured ware, figures were outlined in black on the red ground of the vase and the background was filled in with black. Details were painted in with a brush dipped in clay slip, to create delicate black lines on the red clay ground. This approach gave artists more flexibility than the earlier technique, where details were scratched out of the slipped areas. The figures in red-figured ware became livelier and more natural looking.

These two techniques—black-figured and red-figured—are the ones we think of as most typical of Greek pottery. Athens led the other cities in Greece in production of this ware. By around 500 B.C. Athens was the only Greek city producing and exporting a quantity of finely decorated pottery. Athenian pots have been found far beyond the boundaries of the Greek world.

PROCEDURE

1. Distribute the handout. Show students slides or photographs of both red-figured and black-figured ware, and have them evaluate the differences in style and effect. (In black-figured ware, which depended on incision for detail, the figures tend to look stiff and motionless. In red-figured ware, where details were brushed on, there is a greater sense of movement and naturalism.) At the same time, encourage students to notice the different scenes depicted on the vases. By referring to the handout, they should also be able to identify some common vase shapes.
2. Have students brainstorm a list of scenes from contemporary life that might parallel the scenes they saw on Greek pots. Students should realize that the Greeks considered everything suitable subjects for vase painting.
3. Students choose a scene from their own life to represent in the Greek manner. Encourage them to keep their scenes fairly simple, for ease of execution. One or two figures will be enough for most students to accomplish.
4. Students prepare the outline drawings for their vase paintings. If they wish, they may draw the shape of the "vase" first on the paper, then fit their scene into the open area of the vase. The scene should have a patterned border above and below, either like the Greek ones shown on the handout or a contemporary one.
5. Students paint their scenes using the terra-cotta, black, and white of Greek vases. For students using the black-figured approach, a terra-cotta or white crayon may help them preserve the details in their drawing. Use the crayon to go over the details that the Greeks would have incised into the slip. The wax will resist the water-based paint, leaving the detail area red or white.
6. Display the completed paintings in the classroom.

EXTENSION

Have students search for more information on the Internet. Suggest they begin by using search terms "Ancient Greece," then "art."

Potted History

A lot of what we know about everyday life in ancient Greece comes from Greek pottery. Pottery was an important part of Greek culture. It was one of the few ways people had for holding and carrying liquids. The Greeks did not have plastic or glass, as we do today. They shaped their cups, bowls, and jugs out of clay. Once the clay was fired—heated to a very high temperature—it hardened and kept its shape. It was also fairly waterproof, so containers made of clay could be used to carry liquids.

Greek potters developed different pot shapes for different uses. Here are some of the most common ones.

An *amphora* was used to store and carry liquids (like wine and oil) and solids (like grain and olives). The word *amphora* meant "to carry on both sides." Amphoras always had two vertical handles, a wide body, and a narrow neck.

amphora

hydria

The *hydria* took its name from the Greek word for water. A hydria was used to fetch water from a spring or well. Hydrias usually had oval bodies, two horizontal handles, and one vertical handle.

The name *krater* comes from a word meaning "mix." The krater was a large bowl used for mixing water and wine. (Wine was almost always diluted.) After the water was added, the wine was ladled into cups.

krater

The *kylix* was a wide cup for drinking. It had a shallow bowl and two horizontal handles. The bowl was attached to the foot with a high stem.

kylix

Greek potters used two main styles to decorate their pots. These styles are called **black-figured** and **red-figured painting**. In the black-figured style, the potter painted black figures on the natural red clay. To add details, the painter would scratch through the black coating so that the red clay showed through. Sometimes details were high-lighted with white or dark-red paint.

The red-figured style is the opposite of the black-figured style. In this style, the background of the pot was painted black. The figures were left in the natural red of the clay. Fine black details were painted on with a brush. This style became more popular than the black-figured style because more details could be given.

In both styles, people were shown in an idealized way. Their heads and feet were usually shown in profile, facing sideways. Their upper bodies were usually shown facing out. Sometimes the whole body was shown facing sideways.

(continued)

Potted History *(continued)*

Both styles also included decorative borders above and below the scene. These borders were usually repeating patterns. They included waves, flowers, and a pattern called a Greek key (shown below).

Greek vase painters painted all kinds of scenes on their pots. Some pots show gods and goddesses, or scenes from myths. Some show ordinary people at work: carpenters, leatherworkers, sculptors. And some show scenes from everyday life. There are scenes of miners digging for silver and of laborers gathering olives and pressing grapes for wine. There are scenes of children at school, of ships on the sea, of sporting events, of plays at the theater. There are scenes of battle and scenes of trading, scenes of women in the home, scenes of guests at parties. It is hard to think of any aspect of Greek life that is not shown on Greek pottery.

Greek border patterns

A vase painter at work

How would you show a scene from your life in the style of ancient Greece? Decide on a scene to paint. It can be something from your everyday life—at home or at school—or you can show an event from the world around you: politicians, people at work, a sports event, a concert. To make it easier to draw, don't include too many figures.

If you want, you can set your scene on a standard Greek pottery shape. Draw the shape of the pot on your paper. Fill the whole page with the pot outline. Mark the space on the pot where a scene would usually go. Add a border above and below the scene.

Now draw your scene in the ancient Greek style. Remember that people were usually shown with their heads and legs in profile but with their upper bodies facing forward. Be sure to include a border at the top and bottom of the drawing. You can use a traditional Greek border, like the ones on this page, or you can make up a border of your own.

Choose either the red-figured style or the black-figured style for your painting. In the black-figured style, you will paint the background terra-cotta red, the color of the clay in Greek pots. Your figures will be all black, like silhouettes, with thin red or white lines for details. If you choose the red-figured style, the background will be black and the figures will be terra-cotta red. Details can be added in black.

Homes and Mosaics
in Ancient Athens

OBJECTIVES

Social Studies

- Students will learn of the types of housing available to rich and poor Athenians.

Art

- Students will become familiar with the art of mosaics.
- Students will design and create a simple *mosaic*.

MATERIALS

Homes and Mosaics in Ancient Athens handout

sheets of colored paper, cut into small squares
    (To increase the range of colors and shades available, have students paint sheets of paper in a variety of colors. When the paper is dry, have them cut the sheets into small squares.)

scissors

paper or poster board for base

glue, paste, or glue stick

optional: slides or photographs of Greek mosaics

overhead projector with outline drawing on transparency

translucent colored plastic tiles

BACKGROUND

Since few Greek houses have survived, it is hard to say what a typical Greek house looked like. Much of our information about houses comes from mosaic pictures. Excavations have reconstructed the floor plans of many houses. These tell us how the ground floor of a house was laid out, but tell us nothing about how the rooms were furnished and decorated, or how the rooms on upper stories were laid out.

Then, as now, there was a great difference between the homes of the rich and the poor. In poor homes there were no kitchens. Cooking was done outside over a fire to keep the house from filling with smoke. In winter, when fires were needed indoors for warmth, people simply removed tiles from the roof to create a smoke hole. The houses of the rich had a separate room for cooking.

Although many Athenians owned their homes, some rented them, either because they could not afford to buy a house or because they were not citizens; an Athenian law stated that noncitizens could not own property. If a tenant failed to pay the rent, the landlord often acted to make the house unlivable. This might involve removing the door of the house, taking away the roof tiles, or blocking the tenant's access to the well.

35

Mosaics like those described on the handout were found only in the main rooms of a rich person's home. Some wealthy people even had mosaics installed in their tombs.

PROCEDURE

1. Distribute the handout. If possible, show slides or photographs of Greek mosaics.

2. Using the overhead projector, model filling in an outline drawing with tiles.

3. Distribute mosaic materials. Show students that they can cut their paper tiles to fill in awkward spaces.

4. Students proceed as directed.

5. Display the completed mosaics in the classroom.

VARIATIONS

Tile mosaic

Use small tiles of different colors, either purchased ready-made or made by rolling self-drying clay into thin sheets, then cutting the sheets into small squares, rectangles, and triangles. Use plywood, hardboard, or chipboard as a base.

Pebble mosaic

Gather a quantity of small pebbles, grouped by color and shade. Use wood or plywood as a base.

Duck and griffin

Homes and Mosaics
in Ancient Athens

When you think about buildings in ancient Greece, what images come to mind? A lot of people immediately think of beautiful temples. But temples were built to honor the gods. Ordinary buildings didn't have columns and beautiful carvings. Many of them weren't even made of stone.

The houses most Greek people lived in were very different from these temples. Ordinary homes were made of wood, mud bricks, or stones stuck together with mortar. These houses usually had only two or three rooms. Many of them were so small that their doors had to open to the outside, not the inside. Before going out, people would knock on their own doors from the inside. This warned people walking by to step out of the way. Otherwise the door might hit them when it opened.

The houses of wealthy people were much more comfortable. They were built around an open courtyard, and were often two stories high. On the ground floor there might be a columned entryway, called a *pastas*. This often led to the courtyard and to the living room, or *aule*. The room where men ate and entertained their friends, the *andron*, opened onto the courtyard. The family dining room, or *oikos*, was often next to the kitchen and bathroom. Although all water had to be drawn from a well or carried from a spring, the Greeks believed in regular bathing. The bathroom would include a terra-cotta bath with a drain that led outside, and a wash basin on a stand.

Upstairs were the bedrooms, the slaves' room, and the women's quarters, or *gynaeceum*. Women spent most of their time in this room, spinning, weaving, and visiting with friends. The Greeks thought women should not go out in public, so the wives and daughters of rich men didn't often leave the house. The enclosed courtyard gave them a place to enjoy fresh air in the privacy of their own homes.

Most of the walls in these houses were painted in plain colors. They were often hung with tapestries woven by the women. Some wealthy people had frescoes painted on their walls, but we don't know much about them. Almost none of them have survived. Around the fourth century B.C., a new way of decorating became popula: Rich people had **mosaic** floors put into the main rooms of their houses.

Duck and griffin

At first these mosaics were made using colored pebbles. The artist would sort small pebbles according to their color and shade: light, medium, dark. The pebbles were set in a bed of sand so that they formed a pattern.

(continued)

Homes and Mosaics
in Ancient Athens (continued)

Later mosaics were made using tiles. Since tiles could be made very even in size and shape, and could be made in different colors, mosaics became much more detailed. Some mosaics used such tiny tiles that the finished work looked more like paintings than mosaics. The tiny tiles could be used to create fine details. Some of these mosaics give us valuable information about ancient Greece. Not many houses or boats have survived from Greek times. Yet, Greek mosaic pictures help add to our knowledge of what these looked like in ancient times.

You can use paper to make a Greek-style mosaic.

1. Choose a subject for your mosaic. The subject should be made up of fairly simple shapes. For example, geometric shapes, or animals like fish, cats, and dogs would be good subjects for a mosaic. Busy scenes with lots of people would not be good, because it would be hard to show the details.

2. Draw the outline of your subject on paper or poster board. Fill as much of the paper as you can. The larger you make the image, the easier it will be to work with.

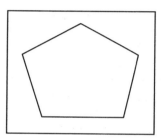
Step 2

3. Now divide the image into smaller areas. Each smaller area will use a different color or a different shade of a color. This will add interest to your mosaic. You should still keep the shapes as simple as you can.

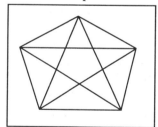
Step 3

4. Starting at the upper edge of your design, coat a small area with glue. Carefully place your paper tiles on the glue. Each tile should be as close as possible to the next tile.

5. When you have finished one area, do the same for a second area. Where areas of different colors meet, or on curves, you can trim your tiles to fit the shape of the edge. Be careful not to lean your hands on an area you have already filled with tiles. Until the glue is completely dry, the pressure could cause the tiles to slip. This is why it is best to start at the top and work down.

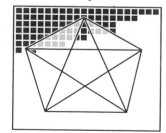
Step 4

6. Continue in this way until all areas have been covered.

Fabulous Frescoes

OBJECTIVES

Social Studies

- Students will learn about the different types of housing available in ancient Rome.

Art

- Students will understand what a fresco is.
- Students will design and paint a fresco.

MATERIALS

Fabulous Frescoes handout
plaster of Paris
water
For each student:
mixing container
shallow foil baking dish (or other disposable container to use as a mold)
watercolor paints and brushes
damp cloths
optional: photographs or slides of Roman frescoes

BACKGROUND

Frescoes—paintings done on wet plaster—were used extensively for decoration in Roman homes. Popular scenes included landscapes, portraits, and scenes from Roman myths.

PROCEDURE

1. Distribute the handout. If possible, show slides of Roman frescoes.

2. Either prepare the plaster blocks in advance, or have students prepare them. If students prepare the plaster, supervise carefully to be sure no plaster is poured down the drain of a sink. The plaster will harden and block the drain. To dispose of plaster, pour any excess into a plastic bag, then wipe out the container with paper towels.

3. Students proceed with frescoes as directed.

4. Display completed frescoes in the classroom.

Fabulous Frescoes

In many big cities today, only rich people own their own homes. Most people live in multistory apartment buildings. Sometimes the ground floors are rented out as shops. Some apartments are big and comfortable, and some are small and cramped. Although the buildings looked different from ours today, this arrangement was also followed in ancient Rome. That's the way cities were back then, too!

By the time of the later republic, most townspeople lived in large apartment blocks called *insulae*. In A.D. 350 a survey of Rome listed 1,790 *domus*, or private homes, and 46,602 *insulae*. For safety, there was a height limit for *insulae*. Only four or five stories were allowed. However, to make more money, landlords often built extra rooms on top. If these were not built well, they made the whole building unsafe.

In typical *insulae*, the rooms at street level were rented out as shops or taverns. Because cooking in apartments was risky—the buildings were made of wood and the only stoves were charcoal braziers, or grills—shops that sold food were popular. A visitor to Rome might also find shops selling clothing, fabric, dishes, and art objects. There were laundries, cleaners, and bakeries, as well as workshops and studios for bronzesmiths, potters, blacksmiths, and furniture makers.

The apartments on the second floor of an *insula* were usually large and comfortable. They were rented by rich people. On the third and fourth floors, the rooms became smaller and shabbier.

Whether they lived in a private house or in an *insula*, wealthy Romans had pleasant homes. The floors were often decorated with mosaics, pictures made from tiny tiles. And the walls were often covered with **frescoes.**

Two lions

These were wall paintings made while the plaster on the wall was still wet. As the paint and plaster dried, they were bonded together. The paint didn't sit on the surface of the wall, it was part of the surface.

Roman artists used paints made from plant and animal dyes. Black came from soot, white from chalk, and some reds and yellows from colored earth. A blue color could be made from copper, and vermilion—a shade of red—was made from a mineral called cinnabar. Other exotic colors were imported as Roman trade routes grew. A really colorful fresco on the wall probably meant that a person was very wealthy—all those colors were very, very expensive.

(continued)

Fabulous Frescoes *(continued)*

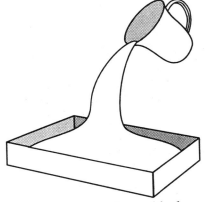

1. To paint your own fresco, you will need a block of plaster. (Plasterboard is coated in paper, so it doesn't work well for painting frescoes.) Mix plaster of Paris by adding the powder to the water. Use about $1\frac{1}{2}$ cups of powder for one cup of water. Stir the mixture thoroughly to remove lumps.

2. Pour the plaster into a baking dish and let it set. Clean out the mixing container by wiping out any remaining plaster with a paper towel and discarding it in the trash. **DO NOT pour any unused plaster down the drain of the sink. It will harden and block the drain.**

Preparing a plaster block

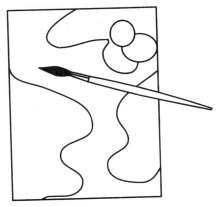

3. When the plaster is firm but still damp, you can start painting your fresco. Choose a pale color, like yellow, for your outlines. Mix it with plenty of water so that the color is very thin. Use this to "draw" the outlines of your design. The colors you use later will cover the yellow, but the lines will act as a guide to get you started.

Painting a fresco

4. If you need to stop work before your fresco is finished, wrap a damp cloth around the plaster. This will keep the plaster from drying out before your painting is done.

5. When your fresco is finished, let the plaster dry completely, then remove the block from the mold.

       Hands-on Culture of Ancient Greece and Rome

Writing in Ancient Rome

OBJECTIVES

Social Studies

- Students will understand how Romans used available technology.
- Students will learn about writing materials used by the Romans.
- Students will use an ancient (early Roman) alphabet.

English/Language Arts

- Students will experience using an earlier version of the Latin alphabet to write English words.

Art

- Students will make their own version of a Roman wax writing tablet.

MATERIALS

Writing in Ancient Rome handout
<u>For each student:</u>
two 8" × 10" rectangles of cardboard
ruler
scissors or craft knife
non-hardening modeling clay
glue
rolling pin
craft stick or clay-modeling tool to use as stylus

PROCEDURE

1. If you wish, you can introduce this activity by asking students what they think people could have used to write on before paper was invented. Then distribute the handout.

2. Students prepare writing tablets as directed on the handout. The tablet may be easier to use if students add two layers of cardboard for the frame. The thicker edge will allow for a deeper layer of clay on the writing surface.

3. When all students have finished their writing tablets, divide class into pairs. Each student should use the early Roman alphabet to write a simple sentence on the tablet, then exchange tablets with a partner and try to read what the partner has written.

Writing in Ancient Rome

Running an empire calls for a lot of paperwork. Unfortunately, the Romans didn't have paper to write on. For permanent records they used papyrus imported from Egypt, or vellum—specially-treated animal skin. Both of these writing materials were expensive. It would be wasteful to use them for taking quick notes or making calculations. And, they certainly couldn't be used in school to teach students to write.

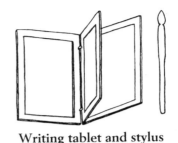

Writing tablet and stylus

When the Romans wanted to write something temporary, they used wooden tablets coated thickly in wax. A pointed stick called a *stylus* was used to make marks in the wax. The other end of the stylus was flat; this was used to smooth out the wax again.

You can use heavy cardboard to make your own version of a wax writing tablet. Cut two 8" × 10" rectangles out of cardboard (figure 1). Use your ruler to draw a one-inch inner frame on one piece of cardboard. Now cut carefully along the lines you have drawn to leave a one-inch cardboard frame (figure 2). Glue this frame to the cardboard rectangle, lining the sides up carefully (figure 3).

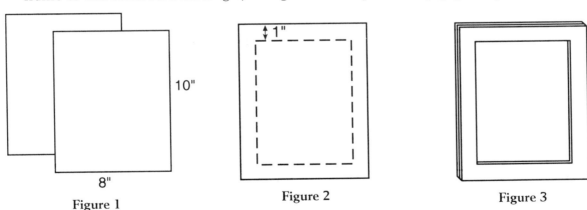

| Figure 1 | Figure 2 | Figure 3 |

Use the rolling pin to roll out a sheet of modeling clay. Measure out a 6" × 8" rectangle in the center of the sheet of clay. Cut out the rectangle and place it inside the cardboard frame of your writing tablet. Starting in the center of the clay, press it firmly in place against the backing. Move gradually out to the edges of the clay. It should fit snugly inside the frame.

(continued)

Writing in Ancient Rome *(continued)*

Now, use the pointed end of your stylus to make letters on the tablet. Try using the early Roman alphabet below to write your own sentence. (You'll notice that the early Roman alphabet didn't use J, K, U, W, Y, or Z. What letters could you use instead?) Trade tablets with a partner. Can you read what your partner's sentence says? When you have finished, you can use the flat end of the stylus to smooth the writing surface out and start again.

Early Roman Alphabet

Games of Ancient Rome

OBJECTIVES

Social Studies
- Students will become familiar with games and pastimes of the ancient Romans.

Math
- Students will create and play a math-based game from another culture.

Art
- Students will create a game board and playing pieces.

MATERIALS

Games of Ancient Rome handout
<u>For each game board:</u>
sheet of 11" × 17" paper or poster board
ruler, pencil, markers
15 black and 15 white playing pieces (game counters, pebbles, beans, etc.)
three dice
Alternatively, a modern backgammon board may be used to play *tabula*.

BACKGROUND

The Romans played a wide variety of board games and other games of chance, often gambling for high stakes. In fact, gambling became such an obsession for many Romans that the government tried to restrict it. Gambling was made illegal except for the weeklong festivities surrounding the festival of Saturnalia.

Like many other government attempts to regulate people's activities, this did not succeed. People continued to gamble. The Emperor Nero himself is said to have played for huge stakes.

The game of *tabula* probably developed out of an earlier game, *ludus duodecim scriptorum*, or "the game of 12 lines." It became popular in Rome during the first century A.D. Emperor Claudius (A.D. 41–54) was fond of the game. He apparently wrote a book on the subject, and had a game board fixed to his chariot so that he could play while traveling.

A later emperor, Zeno (A.D. 475–481), was immortalized by the unlucky throw at *tabula* shown on page 49 of the student handout. Zeno had been in a reasonably good position, with most of his pieces piled so that his opponent could not land on them. Then Zeno rolled 2, 5, 6. The emperor was forced to unpile his *ordinarii*, or piled men, leaving eight uncovered pieces, or blots, on the board. By the time Zeno's move was done it was literally impossible for his opponent to miss hitting one of Zeno's blots. This disastrous throw was still the subject of witticisms half a century later.

PROCEDURE

1. Divide students into pairs. Students should work together as directed on the handout to prepare a *tabula* board. If they wish, they can use Roman motifs to decorate the board.

2. Have students play one or two rounds of the game to become familiar with it. Then suggest that they set up their boards to appear like Zeno's game. Given that no pieces can be taken off the board until all a player's pieces are in the fourth quadrant, and a player must use the whole value of the throw if it can be used, what moves could Zeno make? How many choices did he have? How would the board appear after the move? In fact, Zeno had no choices at all. Each throw could be used, but only by one piece. At the end of Zeno's move, the board looked like this, with Zeno playing white:

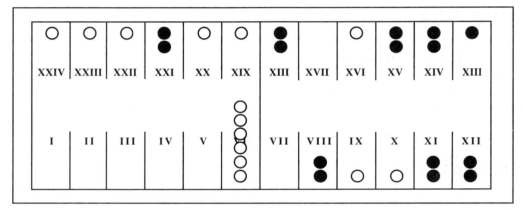

3. Ask students to look at the possible next moves of Zeno's opponent. What combination of numbers would cause Zeno the most damage? What would cause the least damage? Now suggest they return to Zeno's position before his unlucky throw. What would be the best possible throw in this position? Why?

4. Other mathematical investigations with this game might include:

   • In how many different ways can three dice be thrown? (Answer: 56)

   • How many initial moves are possible for the first player when three dice are used? (Answer: 128)

   • What is the least number of throws needed for the first player to win? (Answer: 25 throws)

EXTENSION

Other games students might investigate include *ludum duodecim scripta, latrunculi, tesserae, tali, calculi, felix sex,* and *terni lapilli.* (See the Resources section at the end of this book.)

Have students search for more information on the Internet. Suggest they begin by using search terms "tabula," then "Roman games."

Games of Ancient Rome

What do you think the ancient Romans did for fun? When we think about Romans relaxing, a few things often come to mind: Roman plays in huge stone theaters; gladiator shows and chariot racing.

All these forms of entertainment were certainly popular. But they were big public spectacles. Romans also liked to relax at home, or with friends. Then they often played games similar to jacks, or board games.

One popular board game was called *tabula*. The board was divided into four equal sections. Each player had 15 pieces. The moves were controlled by three six-sided dice.

Both players started at the same point on the board. The aim of the game was to enter all pieces onto the board at one corner, then move all the pieces around the board and take them off at the other end.

At the start of a turn, the player threw all three dice. The numbers thrown could be added together and used for one playing piece, or could be spread out among two or three different pieces. For example, with a roll of 3, 4, and 5, a player would have four choices: move one piece forward 3 spaces, move another piece 4 spaces, and a third piece 5 spaces; or, move one piece 7 spaces (3 + 4) and one piece 5 spaces; move one piece 3 spaces and one piece 9 spaces (4 + 5); or move one piece 12 spaces (3 + 4 + 5).

But, of course, there were obstacles. Both players could not be on the same space at the same time. If one player had two or more pieces on a space, the pieces were called *ordinarii*, or piled men, and the other player could not land on that space. On the other hand, if a player had only one piece on a space, that piece was called a *vagus*. If the other player landed on that space, then the *vagus*, the single piece, was removed from the board. That piece had to enter onto the board again at the starting point, and move all the way around again.

To win, a player had to move all 15 pieces all the way around the board to the fourth quadrant, or section. To remove the pieces from the board, the exact number had to be thrown. So if the player had three pieces on the last space on the board, the only throw that would take a piece off would be a 1. With luck, a player could remove all the pieces quickly. But sometimes the dice would have to be thrown again and again.

An ancient Roman board game

(continued)

Hands-on Culture of Ancient Greece and Rome

Games of Ancient Rome *(continued)*

Try making your own *tabula* board, and play a game from ancient Rome.

1. Draw a one-inch border around a piece of 11" × 17" paper. Draw a line across the middle of the enclosed area, as shown.

2. Draw ten $3\frac{1}{2}$" lines on each edge of the paper, $1\frac{1}{4}$" apart.

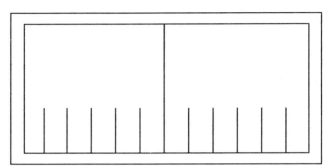

3. Using Roman numerals, number each space. Start with the space in the bottom left, and number it I, the next space II, etc. The bottom right space should be XII. The space above that, at the upper right edge of the board, will be XIII, and the upper left space will be XXIV.

4. All pieces enter from space I and travel counterclockwise. Three dice are thrown, and the three numbers determine the moves of between one and three pieces. Any part of a throw which cannot be used is lost, but a player must use the whole value of the throw if it is possible.

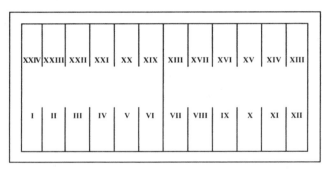

5. If a player lands on a point with one enemy piece, the enemy piece is removed from the board. That piece must then reenter the game (at point I) on the next throw, if possible.

6. If a player has two or more pieces on a point, the other player cannot land on this point, and these pieces cannot be captured. However, these pieces can be skipped over so that the other player can continue moving.

7. No player may enter the second half of the board until all that player's pieces have entered the board.

8. No player can exit the board until all pieces have entered the last quarter. This means that if a single piece is hit, the remaining pieces will be frozen in the last quarter until that piece reenters and moves around to the last quarter again.

(continued)

Games of Ancient Rome (continued)

In the year A.D. 480, the emperor Zeno was playing *tabula*. The board appeared like this, with Zeno playing white:

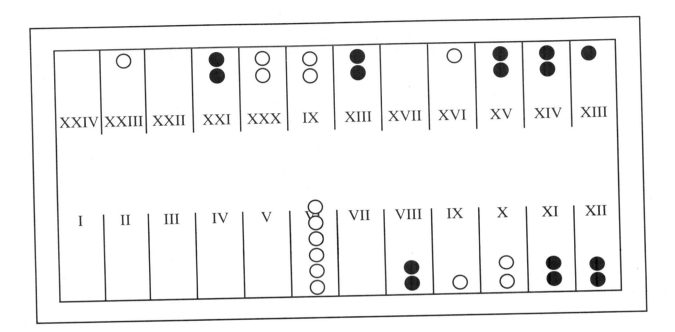

On Zeno's throw, he threw a 2, 5, and 6. The position of the board, and Zeno's throw, were recorded; the throw became famous.

Set up the game on your *tabula* board. Remember, no pieces can be taken off the board until all a player's pieces are in the last quarter, and the full value of the throw must be used if it is possible to use it. What moves could Zeno make? Why do you think this game was recorded?

Hands-on Culture of Ancient Greece and Rome

Living Latin

OBJECTIVES

Social Studies

- Students will understand how the Norman Conquest brought Latin-based words to English.

English/Language Arts

- Students will understand the origin of the Romance languages.
- Students will see the relationship among different Romance languages.
- Students will understand the effect of Latin on English.
- Students will learn the Latin roots of some common English words.
- Students will identify other words based on Latin roots.

MATERIALS

Living Latin handout

BACKGROUND

One of the perquisites of empire-building seems to be imposing your language on the people you conquer. From the sixteenth to the twentieth century, the British imposed English on people from Australia to South Africa. Although the colonies are gone, English remains, used as a *lingua franca* (common language) by people who speak different languages but must interact with each other.

Centuries earlier, the Romans did the same thing. When they conquered an area, they installed a Roman administration. All the business of this administration was conducted in Latin. People in the provinces—the conquered nations—were forced to learn Latin, the language of the Roman Empire. Over the centuries, local dialects of Latin sprang up. Eventually they developed into the distinct, but related, languages we call Romance languages today: French, Spanish, Italian, Portuguese, and Romanian.

Most of the Latin-based words in English today were introduced by the Normans. When William the Conqueror defeated the Saxons in 1066, he brought Norman nobles and ways to England. The French spoken by the Normans mingled with the low German of the Anglo-Saxons and evolved into the language we know now as English.

The Christian Church was another source of Latin-derived words in English. The Latin used by the common people in the Roman Empire was a spoken language, and subject to all the variations and evolutions of spoken language. But the Latin used by the clergy of the Church was a written language, and less liable to change. Just as English was the common language of twentieth-century business, Latin was the common tongue of the clergy until the time of the Reformation. A priest from England and a priest from Antioch could correspond in Latin,

50

though they could not speak each other's native languages. Through them, many Latin words came directly into English, without being modified first by French.

ANSWERS

Matching game:

1. (d)   *per*—through
2. (i)   *respondere*—to answer
3. (a)   *terra*—earth
4. (h)   *video*—I see
5. (c)   *trans*—across
6. (e)   *habere*—to have
7. (j)   *movere*—to move
8. (f)   *femina*—woman
9. (g)   *pugna*—fight
10. (b)   *navigare*—to sail

Students should be able to find hundreds of words based on these Latin words. Some students may need to use a dictionary to identify Latin-based English words. Looking up words that begin with these Latin words should show them how many English words derive from the Latin ones. Here are some possible answers.

per—permeate
respondere—respond
terra—subterranean
video—video
trans—transit
habere—have
movere—movement
femina—feminine
pugna—pugnacious
navigare—navigate

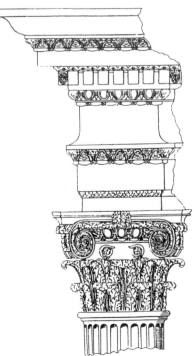

Ornate Roman architecture

Living Latin

When the Romans conquered a new area, they made people learn their language—Latin—and use it to conduct business. After a while people stopped speaking their own languages and just used Latin instead. Even after the Roman Empire collapsed, people continued speaking Latin. Over the centuries the Latin spoken in different areas changed. Gradually, new languages developed. They were based on Latin, but they varied from region to region. These languages include French, Portuguese, Italian, Spanish, and Romanian. Look at the words for the numbers one to five below, and you'll see that these languages are related.

	Latin	**Italian**	**French**	**Spanish**	**Portuguese**	**Romanian**
1.	unus	uno	un	uno	un	un
2.	duo	due	deux	dos	dois	doi
3.	tres	tre	trois	tres	trez	trei
4.	quattor	quattro	quatre	cuatro	quatro	patru
5.	quinque	cinque	cinq	cinco	cince	cinci

Because these languages grew out of the language of the Romans, we call them **Romance languages**. Even though English isn't a Romance language, a lot of our words are based on Latin. You already know a lot of Latin-based words. For example, *lex* means "law" in Latin. The English words "legal" and "legislature" come from it. The Latin word *inter* means "between." The English words "intervene" and "interval" come from it.

Try to recognize the Latin roots for words. They can help you guess the meaning of words you don't know. For example, if you know that the Latin word *magna* means "big," you could guess that "magnificent" has something to with being big.

A Roman classroom

(continued)

Living Latin

Try to match the Latin words on the left with their English meanings on the right.

1. *per*

2. *respondere*

3. *terra*

4. *video*

5. *trans*

6. *habere*

7. *movere*

8. *femina*

9. *pugna*

10. *navigare*

(a) earth

(b) to sail

(c) across

(d) through

(e) to have

(f) woman

(g) fight

(h) I see

(i) to answer

(j) to move

Look carefully at the Latin words in the list above. How many English words can you think of that are based on these words? List as many English words as you can for each Latin word.

_____   _____   _____

_____   _____   _____

_____   _____   _____

_____   _____   _____

_____   _____   _____

_____   _____   _____

_____   _____   _____

Food in Old Rome

OBJECTIVES

Social Studies

- Students will learn about the diets of Romans of different economic levels.
- Students will learn about some of the differences economic standing made to Roman quality of life.
- Students will prepare a simple dish similar to one the Romans ate.

MATERIALS

Food in Old Rome handout
For each group:
1 dozen dates
1 apple
pinch of nutmeg or cinnamon
½ cup nuts
3 tbsp fruit juice
¼ cup unseasoned bread crumbs or graham cracker crumbs

BACKGROUND

In the early days of Rome, a simple diet was the norm for all: coarse bread and wheat porridge were the staples, with a little meat on feast days or after a public sacrifice. In later years, tastes became more elaborate. For wealthy Romans the standard dinner, or *cena*, consisted of at least three courses: the *gustus*, or appetizer; the *cena*, or dinner proper; and the *secunda mensa*, or dessert. The *gustus* consisted of oysters and other shellfish, salted or pickled saltwater fish, uncooked vegetables like onions and lettuce, eggs, and tasty sauces.

The second course, the *cena*, could consist of a number of different dishes. Roman literature gives us the bill of fare of many different meals, from the relatively simple to the extremely elaborate. Juvenal described a meal in which the *gustus* consisted of asparagus and eggs, the *cena* of chicken and goat, and the *secunda mensa* of fruit. Macrobius, writing in the first century A.D., describes a magnificent banquet. The *gustus* was broken into two courses: first, raw sea urchins, oysters, and three kinds of mussels, cooked thrush on asparagus, a fat hen, cooked oysters with mussels; second, mussels again, shellfish, jellyfish, small birds called figpeckers, loin of goat, loin of pork, fricasseed chicken, and two kinds of saltwater snails. The *cena* included sow's udder, boar's head, fish, domesticated duck, wild duck, hare, roast chicken, starch pudding, and bread. Macrobius does not describe the dessert, but surely it, too, was complex and extensive.

PROCEDURE

Divide students into groups of three or four. Distribute the handout and ingredients. Students proceed as directed on the handout.

Food in Old Rome

Italian food. What do you think of when you see these words? Maybe pasta, tomatoes, olives, garlic? Well, in old Rome, you'd be partly right, at least. Olives and garlic were already an important part of Italian cooking. But tomatoes were found only in the Americas, still unknown to Europe, and pasta had not yet been developed. Instead, most early Romans ate various kinds of bread, and a kind of porridge made of wheat.

Rich people had a more varied diet. For them, vegetables included artichokes, asparagus, beans, beets, cabbage, cucumbers, lentils, onions, and peas. Goat, beef, mutton, and pork were available for meat, as well as poultry of all sorts. Fish and shellfish were very popular—fresh, dried, and salted. And, of course, olives and olive oil have long been essential elements of Italian cooking.

Wealthy Romans had large kitchens where their slaves often prepared elaborate meals. But most Romans had no kitchens at all. In fact, home cooking was often against the law. At that time the only stoves available were charcoal braziers. These were similar to the charcoal grills we enjoy in the summer. But, of course, these stoves were used indoors. Since many Romans lived in apartment buildings made largely of wood, the charcoal stoves presented a real risk of fire. So various emperors passed laws that made it illegal for ordinary Romans to cook at home. (Of course the rich, with their stone houses and separate kitchens, weren't affected by these laws.)

Instead, most Romans bought a lot of their food ready-made from shops and stalls in the market. They also developed recipes for dishes that could be made without cooking.

The ancient Romans could have made this recipe for stuffed dates without a kitchen.

Stuffed Dates

1 dozen dates (pitted if possible)

1 apple

pinch of nutmeg or cinnamon

$\frac{1}{2}$ cup shelled nuts

3 tbsp fruit juice

$\frac{1}{4}$ cup unseasoned bread crumbs or graham cracker crumbs

Chop up the apple and nuts. Mix them together with the nutmeg or cinnamon and bread crumbs or graham cracker crumbs. Add enough fruit juice to moisten the mixture.

Cut the tops off the dates and remove the pits (if necessary). Push the filling in with a spoon. Arrange the dates attractively on a serving plate.

Roman Proverbs and Sayings

OBJECTIVES

Social Studies
- Students will understand some of the commonalities among different cultures.
- Students will understand that proverbs and sayings can be used to transmit culture.

English/Language Arts
- Students will analyze the meaning of unfamiliar phrases to find parallels with English phrases.
- Students will learn that proverbs can carry the wisdom of people from generation to generation.

MATERIALS
Roman Proverbs and Sayings handout

BACKGROUND

Proverbs are part of every spoken language. Comparing proverbs from different parts of the world shows that the same kernel of wisdom can be expressed in different ways. Proverbs often reflect the different cultures that develop them. Many proverbs form part of a code of behavior and are used to transmit rules of conduct within a culture. They also tend to use rhyme, alliteration, and homely imagery—household objects, animals, and the events of everyday life. Some sayings that originated in Roman times are still common today; students may be surprised to find the origin of some common proverbs. Here are some Roman sayings, their translations, and current English proverbs that have a similar meaning.

Caelum, non animum, mutant qui trans mare currunt. (Horace)
Those who cross the sea change their environment, not themselves.
The leopard cannot change his spots.

Fames est optimus coquus.
Hunger is the best cook.
Hunger is the best sauce.

Tanto brevis omne quanto felicius tempus. (Pliny the Younger)
The happier a time is, the shorter it seems.
Time flies when you're having fun.

Dimidium facti qui coepit habet. (Horace)
He who has begun has the job half done.
Well begun, half done.

PROCEDURE

1. Distribute the handout and discuss it with students. If you want, you can use some of the proverbs given in the Background section as examples while you model the process.

2. Students proceed as directed on the handout.

ANSWERS

Many choices are possible; here are some English versions of the Roman proverbs and sayings students might choose.

1. It takes one to know one.

2. Love is blind.

3. Truth is stranger than fiction.

4. United we stand, divided we fall.

5. The big fish in a small pond is a small fish in a big pond.

EXTENSION

Have students choose one proverb to illustrate. The illustration can be set in early Rome, or in modern times.

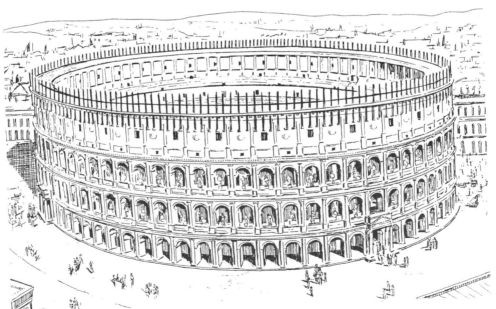

The Colosseum in Rome, completed A.D. 80

 # Roman Proverbs and Sayings

Proverbs are short, clever sayings. They use picturesque language to express a piece of wisdom. All cultures have developed proverbs. In fact, some proverbs we use today have been in use for centuries. Some were probably even used in Roman times.

Here are some Roman proverbs—first given in Latin and then translated into English. See if you can think of a contemporary proverb that means about the same thing as each translated Roman one. If you can't think of a modern proverb with a similar meaning, reword these proverbs to sound like ones people could use today.

1. *Furum fur cognoscit et lupum lupis.*

   A thief recognizes a thief and a wolf a wolf.

   _____

2. *Nemo in amore videt.*

   No one in love sees.

   _____

3. *In omni re vincit imitationem veritas.*

   In everything truth conquers imitation.

   _____

4. *Ibi semper est victoria ubi concordia est.*

   Where there is cooperation there is always victory.

   _____

5. *Navis, quae in flumine magna est, in mari parvula est.*

   The ship that is big in the river is small in the ocean.

   _____

Roman Numerals

OBJECTIVES

Math

- Students will recognize Roman numerals as numbers.
- Students will identify each Roman numeral symbol and its Indo-Arabic value.
- Students will be able to convert Roman numerals into Indo-Arabic numbers.
- Students will be able to convert Indo-Arabic numbers into Roman numerals.
- Students will understand some of the difficulties of calculating using Roman numerals.

Social Studies

- Students will understand that different cultures develop different responses to the same needs.
- Students will learn some history of the Roman numeral system.

MATERIALS

Roman Numerals handout
flat toothpicks or other small manipulative

PROCEDURE

1. Distribute the handout. Draw some Roman numerals on the board or overhead. Ask students if they are familiar with these symbols.

2. Students proceed as directed on the handout.

ANSWERS

Forming Roman numerals:

5	V	49	XLIX
9	IX	135	CXXXV
6	VI	1941	MCMXLI
14	XIV	4357	M$\overline{\text{V}}$XXXLVII

Here is the completed table:

Roman Numerals and their Indo-Arabic Equivalents									
1	I	11	XI	10	X	100	C	1000	M
2	II	12	XII	20	XX	200	CC	2000	MM
3	III	13	XIII	30	XXX	300	CCC	3000	MMM
4	IV	14	XIV	40	XL	400	CD	4000	$M\overline{V}$
5	V	15	XV	50	L	500	D	5000	$\overline{V}$
6	VI	16	XVI	60	LX	600	DC	6000	$\overline{VI}$
7	VII	17	XVII	70	LXX	700	DCC	7000	$\overline{VII}$
8	VIII	18	XVIII	80	LXXX	800	DCCC	8000	$\overline{VIII}$
9	IX	19	XIX	90	XC	900	CM	9000	$\overline{IX}$

Adding Roman numerals:
1. CXXI + CXII = CCXXXIII (121 + 112 = 233)
2. XVI + VII = XXIII (16 + 7 = 23)
3. CXII + XII = CXXIV (112 + 12 = 124)
4. XIV + VII = XXI (14 + 7 = 21)
5. XCVI + XIV = CX (96 + 14 = 110)

Roman numerals today:

Uses include clock and watch faces, movie and book copyright dates, dates inscribed on buildings, front-matter page numbers in books

EXTENSION

Have students search for more information on the Internet. Suggest they begin by using the following search terms: "number," "numeration," "history of math."

Roman Numerals

The number system we use today was first developed in India. Traders from Arabia saw how useful the system could be, and brought it back to the Mediterranean area. Finally, Europeans learned of the system from Muslims in Spain. Soon Europeans were using this system, too. Because these numbers came from India through Arabia, we call them **Indo-Arabic numbers**.

But what kind of numbers did people in Europe use before Indo-Arabic numbers were introduced? They used **Roman numerals**. The Roman numeral system was developed around 500 B.C. It was based on an earlier Greek system. Roman numerals use seven letters to stand for certain values:

I = 1	C = 100
V = 5	D = 500
X = 10	M = 1000
L = 50	

To show other values, the letter symbols were combined. Both addition and subtraction were used in combining symbols. If the same symbol was repeated two or three times, the values were added:

$$III = I + I + I \quad (= 1 + 1 + 1 = 3)$$
$$XX = X + X \quad (= 10 + 10 = 20)$$

If two different symbols were combined with the larger value on the left and the smaller one on the right, the values were **added**:

$$XV = X + V \quad (= 10 + 5 = 15)$$
$$XVI = X + V + I \quad (= 10 + 5 + 1 = 16)$$

If two different symbols were combined with the smaller value on the left and the larger one on the right, then the smaller value was seen as a negative. It was **subtracted** from the larger one:

$$IV = -I + V = V - I \quad (= 5 - 1 = 4)$$
$$IX = -I + X = X - I \quad (= 10 - 1 = 9)$$

The Roman system only included symbols for numbers up to 1000. If people wanted to write a larger number, they used a bar over the symbol. The bar meant "multiply by 1000."

$$\overline{V} = 5 \ (1000) = 5000$$
$$\overline{X} = 10 \ (1000) = 10{,}000$$
$$\overline{D} = 500 \ (1000) = 500{,}000$$
$$\overline{M} = 1000 \ (1000) = 1{,}000{,}000$$

(continued)

Roman Numerals *(continued)*

Here is a simplified version of the rules for reading and writing Roman numerals.

1. A lesser number before a greater number is negative: IX = –I + X

2. A symbol can be repeated only three times. Then a different symbol must be used, combining subtraction as well as addition. So we can write 3 as III, but 4 can't be written as IIII. It must be written as IV.

3. Two negative symbols cannot be used together. You cannot write 8 as IIX.

4. The symbol I can be used only as a negative before V or X.

5. The symbol X can be used only as a negative before L or C.

6. There is no Roman numeral for zero.

7. A bar over a letter means "multiply by 1000."

Use toothpicks to form the Roman numeral equivalents of these numbers:

5	49
9	135
6	1941
14	4357

To read a Roman numeral, **start at the left**. As long as the symbols are in descending order of value, add the values together. If a smaller value comes before a larger value—for example, IV, IX, XL, XC, CD, or CM—subtract the smaller value from the larger value. Then add the values together.

MCMLXXXVI = M + (M – C) + L + X + X + X + V + I
= 1000 + (1000 – 100) + 50 + 10 + 10 + 10 + 5 + 1
= 1000 + 900 + 50 + 10 + 10 + 10 + 5 + 1
= 1986

(continued)

Roman Numerals *(continued)*

Here is a table showing Roman numerals and their Indo-Arabic equivalents. Complete the table by filling in the blank squares.

Roman Numerals and Their Indo-Arabic Equivalents									
1	I	11	XI	10	X	100	C	1000	M
2	II	12		20		200	CC	2000	MM
3		13	XIII	30	XXX	300		3000	
4	IV	14		40	XL	400	CD	4000	$\overline{MV}$
5	V	15	XV	50		500		5000	$\overline{V}$
6		16	XVI	60	LX	600	DC	6000	$\overline{VI}$
7	VII	17		70	LXX	700		7000	$\overline{VII}$
8	VIII	18	XVIII	80	LXXX	800	DCCC	8000	$\overline{VIII}$
9	IX	19	XIX	90	XC	900		9000	

Now that you are familiar with the way Roman numerals are written, try using them to do simple calculations. Add the following numbers together. Write the sum in Roman numerals.

1. CXXI + CXII =

2. XVI + VII =

3. CXII + XII =

4. XIV + VII =

5. XCVI + XIV =

If you found these numbers hard to add, you're not alone. A lot of people find it easiest to change the Roman numerals into Indo-Arabic ones, add them up, then change the sum back into Roman numerals. The Roman numeral system worked well for writing numbers down, but the numerals were hard to work with. That's probably why the Indo-Arabic system was adopted so quickly. It was much, much easier to use.

Even so, Roman numerals still have their uses. Can you think of any places where you might see Roman numerals? List as many of them as you can.

_____   _____

_____   _____

_____   _____

A Roman Calculator

OBJECTIVES

Social Studies

- Students will learn how the Romans performed calculations despite their cumbersome numeral system.

Math

- Students will use a simple abacus to perform calculations.
- Students will convert Roman numerals to Indo-Arabic, and vice versa.

Art

- Students will create a working paper abacus.

English/Language Arts

- Students will become aware of the effect of Latin on English.

MATERIALS

A Roman Calculator handout
overhead projector
For each abacus:
paper or poster board
ruler
drawing materials
20 small counters

PREPARATION

Use the diagram on the student page to prepare an overhead transparency of a Roman abacus. Students should be familiar with Roman numerals and notation. The activity on Roman numerals, page 59, is a good introduction to this one.

PROCEDURE

1. Distribute the handout. Discuss the difficulties of performing calculations using Roman numerals. Students prepare their abaci as directed on the handout.

2. Demonstrate the use of the abacus on the overhead projector. Students should understand that one counter in a groove stands for one of that groove's value, e.g., one counter in the X groove stands for one X, or 10.

3. Show how to add numerals on the abacus. Explain the process of simplifying the answer.

4. Students prepare their own addition problems and work them on the abacus.

5. The same procedure can be used for subtracting on the abacus. If you wish, you can ask students how they think subtraction would be done. Students should prepare their own subtraction problems and work them on the abacus.

ANSWERS

XXXI + LXXI = CII   (31 + 71 = 102)

XXIII + LVIII = LXXXI   (23 + 58 = 81)

CXLII + LXVIII = CCX   (142 + 68 = 210)

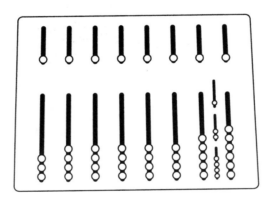

Abacus

A Roman Calculator

The Roman numeral system is efficient in a way. It uses just seven letters to express all numbers. But it makes calculations difficult. Even simple addition, like VII + VIII (7 + 8) calls for more carrying and converting than it does in our system. So, how did the Romans do the calculations they needed for all those roads, aqueducts, and monumental buildings?

They used an early version of the **abacus**. At its simplest, this abacus was just grooves scratched in the dust. Pebbles were put in the grooves. They could be moved from groove to groove to add and subtract numbers. A more permanent abacus was made by carving grooves in a piece of wood. In this activity, you will use paper to make your own version of a Roman abacus.

1. Copy the abacus pattern in figure 1 onto a piece of paper or poster board. The shaded areas stand for the grooves in the original abacus. Label each "groove" as shown.

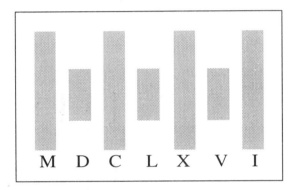

Figure 1: Pattern for Roman Abacus

2. To show a number on the abacus, put one counter in the appropriate place for each letter in the numeral. For example, to show XVII, you would put one counter in the X groove, one in the V groove, and two in the I groove. (See figure 2.)

Practice using the abacus. Show each of these numerals on your abacus.

DCLXVI

CCLXVII

CLXXXVII

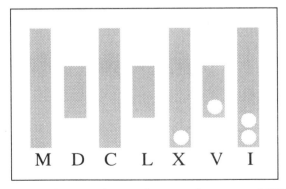

Figure 2: Roman abacus showing the numeral XVII

(continued)

Name _____   Date _____

A Roman Calculator (continued)

Now try adding some numbers. To add two numbers on the abacus, show the first number on the abacus with your counters. Now add counters to show the second number, as well.

XVI + XVII

The sum is shown by the total number of counters in each groove:

XXVVIII

Now you'll have to simplify. There are two counters in the V groove. But when you write Roman numerals you wouldn't write VV, you'd write X. So you can convert the two V's into one X. Take the counters out of the V groove. Put one in the X groove and put the other one back in your pile.

Now write out the numeral shown on the abacus. Write each symbol once for every counter in that groove.

XXXIII

The rule to remember when simplifying is that you should never have more than four counters in a long groove, except for the M groove. You should never have more than one counter in a short groove. Five I's can be converted into one V. Two V's can be converted into one X, five X's into an L, and so on.

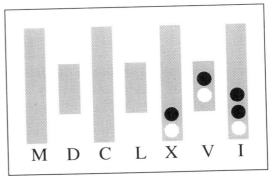

White counters show XVI, black ones show XVII.

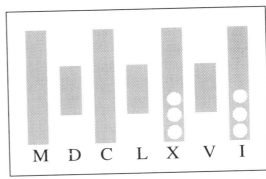

Simplify by converting two V's into one X.

Practice adding with these numbers. Then simplify the results. Write the sum in Roman numerals.

XXXI + LXXI =
XXIII + LVIII =
CXLII + LXVIII =

You can use the same method for adding more than two numerals. Write out some Roman numeral addition problems using three or more numerals. Now do your problems using the abacus. Be careful when you're writing 4 and 9 in Roman numerals—they're IV and IX, not IIII or VIIII.

Note: The Latin word for the pebbles used on the abacus was *calculi*. Our word "calculate" comes from this. So the Roman abacus really was the world's first *calculator*.

© 1998 J. Weston Walch, Publisher

Hands-on Culture of Ancient Greece and Rome

Resources

GREECE

General

Blaisdell, Bob. *Favorite Greek Myths*. New York: Dover Publications, Inc., 1995.

Burrell, Roy, and Peter Connolly. *The Greeks*. New York: Oxford University Press, 1990.

Coolidge, Oliver. *Golden Days of Greece*. New York: Harper Junior Books, 1990.

Descamps-Lequime, Sophie, and Denise Vernerey. *Peoples of the Past: The Ancient Greeks*. Brookfield, CT: The Millbrook Press, 1992.

Freeman, Charles. *Spotlights: The Ancient Greeks*. New York: Oxford University Press, 1996.

Honan, Linda. *Spend the Day in Ancient Greece: Projects and Activities That Bring the Past to Life*. New York: John Wiley & Sons, Inc. 1998.

MacDonald, Fiona. *How Would You Survive as an Ancient Greek?* Danbury, CT: Franklin Watts, 1995.

MacDonald, Fiona, and Mark Bergin. *Inside Story: A Greek Temple*. New York: Peter Bedrick Books, 1992.

Peach, Susan, and Anne Millard. *The Usborne Illustrated World History: The Greeks*. Tulsa, OK: EDC Publishing, 1995.

Pearson, Anne. *Ancient Greece*, Eyewitness Books. New York: Knopf, 1992.

Powell, Anton. *Cultural Atlas for Young People: Ancient Greece*. New York: Facts on File, 1989.

Schomp, Virginia. *Cultures of the Past: The Ancient Greeks*. Tarrytown, NY: Benchmark Books, 1996.

Perseus. New Haven, CT: Yale University Press, 1993. CD-ROM and videodisc of Greek texts and art.

http://history.evansville.net/greece.html

Potted History

http://harpy.uccs.edu/greek/grkpots.html

ROME

General

Altman, John. *Ancient Rome*. Carthage, IL: Good Apple, 1991.

Bell, Robbie, and Michael Cornelius. *Board Games Round the World: A Resource Book for Mathematical Investigations*. New York: Cambridge University Press, 1988.

Bell, R.C. *Board and Table Games from Many Civilizations*. New York: Dover Publications Inc., 1979.

Caselli, Giovanni. *History of Everyday Things: The Roman Empire and the Dark Ages*. New York: Peter Bedrick Books, 1981.

Corbishley, Mike. *Everyday Life in Roman Times*. New York: Franklin Watts, 1994.

Ganeri, Anita. *How Would You Survive as an Ancient Roman?* Danbury, CT: Franklin Watts, 1995.

Guittard, Charles, and Annie-Claude Martin. *Peoples of the Past: The Romans—Life in the Empire*. Brookfield, CT: The Millbrook Press, 1992.

Haslam, Andrew. *Make It Work: The Roman Empire*. Chicago, IL: World Book, Inc., 1996.

Haywood, John. *Spotlights: The Romans*. New York: Oxford University Press, 1996.

Marks, Anthony, and Graham Tingay. *The Usborne Illustrated World History: The Romans*. Tulsa, OK: EDC Publishing, 1994.

Morley, Jacqueline, and John James. *Inside Story: A Roman Villa*. New York: Peter Bedrick Books, 1992.

Robinson, Charles Alexander, Jr. *Ancient Rome: A First Book*. New York: Franklin Watts, 1984.

Games of Ancient Rome

www.personal.psu.edu/users/w/x/wxk116/roma/rbgames.html

Bell, R.C. *Board and Table Games from Many Civilizations*. New York: Dover Publications, 1979.

Glossary

abacus	simple device used to perform mathematical calculations
agora	marketplace or general meeting place
amphora	large jar with two handles used to store and carry liquids, like wine and oil, and solids, like grain and olives
andron	(Greek: ανδρον) room where men ate and entertained their friends
anthropos	(Greek: ανθροπος) human
anti	(Greek: αντι) against
archae	(Greek: αρχαι) ancient
Archaic Period	800 B.C.–650 B.C.
Assembly	(Greek: εκκλεσια) the parliament of Athens where citizens met to discuss the city's affairs
astro	(Greek: αστρο) star
aule	(Greek: αυλε) living room in Greek home
auto	(Greek: αυτο) self
bios	(Greek: βιος) life
black-figured ware	vase-painting style featuring black figures against a red background
bouleterion	(Greek: βουλετεριον) council of Athens; 500 citizens, 50 from each tribe, chosen by lot
brazier	charcoal grill used by Romans for cooking
calculi	(Latin) pebbles used on Roman abacus; origin of our words *calculate, calculator*; Roman board game
capital	carved stone top of a column
cena	(Latin) dinner
chorus	(Greek: χοροσ) in Greek drama, group of actors who chanted songs or filled in background of play
chrono	(Greek: χρονο) time
citizen	a free man who had the right to participate in the government of his city-state
clay slip	thin mixture of clay and water used to decorate pottery

Cleisthenes	Athenian who introduced first democratic government
column	tall, cylindrical pillar made of stone
Corinth	(Greek: Κορινθ) Greek city-state
courtyard	central area left open to the air around which Greek and Roman houses were built
cycle	(Grreek: κυκλοω) circle
demes	smallest division of Athenian city-state, subdivision of *trittyes*
demokratia	democracy, system of government where people make own decisions about affairs
demos	(Greek: δεμος) people
drama	(Greek: δραμα) a play
duo	(Greek: δυο) two
dynami	(Greek: δυναμι) power, force
ecclesia	(Greek: εκκλησια) assembly, composed of all citizens of Athens
felix sex	(Latin) board game
femina	(Latin) woman
fresco	wall painting done while plaster was still wet, so that the pigment became a part of the wall
geo	(Greek: γεω) earth
Geometric style	early vase-painting style, including triangles and squares in alternating colors
grapho	(Greek: γραφω) I draw, write
gustus	Roman appetizer
gynaeceum	women's quarters in Greek home
habere	(Latin) to have
hydor	(Greek: 'υδορ) water
hydria	(Greek: 'υδρια) jar used to fetch water from a spring or well; hydrias usually had oval bodies, two horizontal handles, and one vertical handle
hyper	(Greek: 'υπερ) above, beyond
idea	(Greek: ιδεα) notion
inter	(Latin) between
juror	member of committee who listened to criminal cases, decided on guilt or innocence of accused

Juvenal	Roman author
krater	(Greek: κρατηρ) large bowl used for mixing water and wine
kratos	(Greek: κρατος) strength, power, government
kylix	(Greek: κυλιξ) wide cup for drinking, with a shallow bowl and two horizontal handles; the bowl was attached to the foot with a high stem
latrunculi	(Latin) board game
lex	(Latin) law
lingua franca	common language used by people who speak different languages but must interact with each other
ludus duodecim scriptorum	(Latin) board game, the game of 12 lines
Macrobius	Roman author
macros	(Greek: μακρος) large
magna	(Latin) big
Martial	Roman author
mega	(Greek: μεγα) big
meter	measure
micros	(Greek: μικρος) small
monos	(Greek: μονος) single, alone
mosaic	picture made of small colored tiles or pebbles
Mount Olympus	mountain in northern Greece where Greeks believed gods lived
movere	(Latin) to move
myth	traditional fictional story, usually involving divine beings, that explains the customs or beliefs of a people
mythos	(Greek: μυθος) story
navigare	(Latin) to sail
oikos	(Greek: οικος) family dining room in Greek home, house, home
-ology	study, science
oracle	sacred place where people went to consult a god or goddess
ordinarii	(Latin) piled men in the game of tabula
Orientalizing style	early vase-painting style, angular geometric patterns of earlier periods softened

ostracism	Athenian practice of exiling politicians for 10 years based on popular vote
ostrakon, ostrakei	(Greek: οστρακον, plural οστρακει) piece of broken pottery used in vote to exile politician; origin of English word *ostracize*
papyrus	writing material made from reeds, imported from Egypt
pastas	(Greek: παστας) columned entryway in Greek home
pebble mosaic	mosaic made using colored pebbles
per	(Latin) through
phobos	(Greek: φοβος) fear
phono	(Greek: φονο) sound
phylae	(Greek: φυλαι) tribes, division of Athenian city-state; 10 tribes, each made up of three *trittyes*, one from the city, one from the country, one from the coast
Pnyx	"the crowded place," hill opposite the Acropolis in Athens where meetings of the Assembly were held
polis	(Greek: πολις) independent Greek state consisting of a city and the surrounding countryside
poly	(Greek: πολυ) many
Proto-Geometric	early vase-painting style, concentric circles and semi-circles, augmented with simple zigzags and wavy lines
proverb	short, clever saying
provinces	nations conquered by Rome and incorporated into the Empire
pugna	(Latin) fight
red-figured ware	vase-painting style featuring red figures against a black background
respondere	(Latin) to answer
Romance language	language based on Latin: French, Spanish, Italian, Portuguese, and Romanian
Saturnalia	(Latin) festival celebrated with a week of festivities
scopeo	(Greek: σκοπεω) I look
secunda mensa	(Latin) dessert
sesterces	(Latin) unit of money

strategos, strategoi	(Greek: στρατεγος, στρατεγοι) Athenian army commander, elected annually
stylus	pointed stick used to make marks in wax writing tablet
syn, sym	(Greek: συν, συμ) together
tabula	(Latin) board game
tali	(Latin) board game
tapestry	woven wall hanging
tele	(Greek: τελε) far
terni lapilli	(Latin) board game
terra	(Latin) earth
tesserae	(Latin) board game
therm	(Greek: θερμ) heat
thesis	(Greek: θεσυς) proposition
trans	(Latin) across
trittyes	division of Athenian city-state; 30 in all, 10 from the coast, 10 from the city, and 10 from the country
tyrant	(Greek: τυραντ) ruler, someone who governed with absolute power
underworld	the land of the dead, which the Greeks called Hades
vellum	specially treated animal skin, used as writing material
video	(Latin) I see
word root	the essential part of a word used to form other words
writing tablet	wax-covered board used by Greeks and Romans as writing surface
Zeno	Roman emperor noted for a disastrous throw at tabula